# Lecture Notes
# in Business Information Processing 451

Series Editors

Wil van der Aalst ⓘ
*RWTH Aachen University, Aachen, Germany*

John Mylopoulos ⓘ
*University of Trento, Trento, Italy*

Sudha Ram ⓘ
*University of Arizona, Tucson, AZ, USA*

Michael Rosemann ⓘ
*Queensland University of Technology, Brisbane, QLD, Australia*

Clemens Szyperski
*Microsoft Research, Redmond, WA, USA*

More information about this series at https://link.springer.com/bookseries/7911

Jennifer Horkoff · Estefania Serral ·
Jelena Zdravkovic (Eds.)

# Advanced Information Systems Engineering Workshops

CAiSE 2022 International Workshops
Leuven, Belgium, June 6–10, 2022
Proceedings

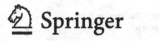

*Editors*
Jennifer Horkoff 🆔
Chalmers | University of Gothenburg
Gothenburg, Sweden

Estefania Serral 🆔
KU Leuven
Brussels, Belgium

Jelena Zdravkovic 🆔
Stockholm University
Stockholm, Sweden

ISSN 1865-1348                     ISSN 1865-1356 (electronic)
Lecture Notes in Business Information Processing
ISBN 978-3-031-07477-6       ISBN 978-3-031-07478-3 (eBook)
https://doi.org/10.1007/978-3-031-07478-3

This Springer imprint is published by the registered company Springer Nature Switzerland AG
The registered company address is: Gewerbestrasse 11, 6330 Cham, Switzerland

# Preface

Over the last two decades, the Conference on Advanced Information Systems Engineering (CAiSE) has been established as a leading venue for information systems engineering research on innovative topics with rigorous scientific theories. The theme of this year's CAiSE, "Information systems in the post-COVID era: reconciling the best of both worlds", emphasized the challenge of "going back to normal" and what has been learned from about the two years of digital experiences triggered by the pandemic. The theme also reflected the conference organization – after the online editions of CAiSE 2020 and 2021, this year the conference returned as a live event held during June 6–10, 2022, in Leuven, Belgium. Each year CAiSE is accompanied by a significant number of high-quality workshops. Their aim is to address specific emerging challenges in the field, to facilitate interaction between stakeholders and researchers, to discuss innovative ideas, and to present new approaches and tools. Two kinds of workshops were invited:

- Presentation-oriented workshops focused on presentations and discussions of accepted papers. These papers are published in this Springer LNBIP volume.
- Discussion-oriented workshops emphasized discussions facilitated by paper presentations. The main criterion for paper acceptance was relevance and potential for raising discussion, and as such these papers are not published in this Springer LNBIP volume.

Initially, 12 workshops were accepted; the challenges of the post-COVID period, including the uncertainty about the conference organization, led to 65 submissions and six workshops finally succeeding with a sufficient number of high-quality accepted papers. The workshops reflected a broad range of exciting topics and trends ranging from blockchain technologies via digital factories, ethics, and ontologies to the agile methods for business and information systems. Specifically, this volume contains the proceedings of the following presentation-oriented workshops (which received 23 submissions and accepted 11 papers):

- The 2nd International Workshop on Blockchain for Information Systems (BC4IS)
- The 2nd International Workshop on Information Systems Engineering for Smarter Life (ISESL)
- The 4th International Workshop on Key Enabling Technologies for Digital Factories (KET4DF)

The 2nd International Workshop on Model-driven Organizational and Business Agility (MOBA) received 22 submissions and published post-proceedings in a separate LNBIP volume. Regarding the discussion-oriented workshops, the 16th International Workshop on Value Modelling and Business Ontologies (VMBO) received 12 submissions, and the 1st International Workshop on Agile Methods for Information Systems Engineering (Agil-ISE) received seven submissions. Being discussion-oriented, they opted to publish their proceedings in the CEUR Workshop Proceedings series. We would like to thank the chairs of the workshops for their excellent job in difficult times. Also, we thank the reviewers for their timely and constructive work, as well as the publicity chairs for their numerous activities that helped attract submissions. We thank Springer for the swift communication and support of the proceedings production process. Finally, we warmly thank Monique Snoeck and Frederik Gailly—the General Co-chairs of CAiSE 2022—for continuously helping us in the process.

June 2022

Jelena Zdravkovic
Jennifer Horkoff
Estefania Serral

# Organization

**CAiSE Workshops Chairs**

Jennifer Horkoff            Chalmers University and University of
                               Gotenburg, Sweden
Estefania Serral            KU Leuven, Belgium
Jelena Zdravkovic           Stockholm University, Sweden

# Contents

# BC4IS 2022

# Second International Workshop on Blockchain for Information Systems (BC4IS 2022)

## Preface

Blockchain technology offers a wide variety of opportunities to enable new kinds of collaborations and organizations, and to improve existing ones. However, engineering blockchain-based systems is a task that is particularly complex, and that requires specific considerations, along with more traditional information systems engineering questions. In this context, research around the definition of requirements for, development, use, and evolution of blockchain-based information systems is particularly relevant.

These opportunities and challenges have generated a strong and continuously growing interest from industry and academia in the engineering of blockchain-based information systems. To help further expand knowledge around this technology and to provide relevant answers to blockchain-specific engineering questions, we organized the second edition of the Blockchain for Information Systems (BC4IS) workshop.

The workshop was held in conjunction with the 34th International Conference on Advanced Information Systems Engineering (CAiSE 2022). It is a well-established and highly visible conference series, addressing contemporary topics in information systems engineering.

We invited researchers working in fields including conceptual modeling, ontology engineering, business process modeling and analysis, and information systems to submit their contributions to the workshop. Four papers were submitted, and each received two single blind reviews. A meta-review of each paper was then prepared by the workshop chairs and sent to the authors. Taking into consideration the reviews and the maximum acceptance rate at, two papers were accepted and presented during the workshop.

Considering the ongoing pandemic, the first edition of the workshop had to be organized remotely. This year, we were very excited to hold the workshop physically in Leuven. We also had the chance to have a compelling keynote, given by Wim Laurier on the topic of "The Ontological Dimensions of Blockchain Initiatives", attracting both blockchain aficionados and non-experts.

As chairs of the BC4IS workshop, we would like to express our gratitude to the chairs of the CAiSE conference, to all the people that contributed to the organization of the workshop, and to the authors for their valuable contributions. We are looking forward to meeting again at the third edition of BC4IS in 2023!

June 2022
Sarah Bouraga
Victor Amaral de Sousa
Corentin Burnay

# Organization

## Workshop Organizers

| | |
|---|---|
| Sarah Bouraga | University of Namur, Belgium |
| Victor Amaral de Sousa | University of Namur, Belgium |
| Corentin Burnay | University of Namur, Belgium |

## Workshop Steering Committee

| | |
|---|---|
| Monique Snoeck | KU Leuven, Belgium |
| Stéphane Faulkner | University of Namur, Belgium |
| Ivan J. Jureta | FNRS and University of Namur, Belgium |
| Wim Laurier | University of Saint-Louis - Brussels, Belgium |

## Program Committee

| | |
|---|---|
| Monique Snoeck | KU Leuven, Belgium |
| Pierluigi Plebani | Polytechnic University of Milan, Italy |
| Ghareeb Falazi | University of Stuttgart, Germany |
| Nicolas Six | University of Paris 1 Panthéon-Sorbonne, France |
| Orlenys López-Pintado | University of Tartu, Estonia |
| Wim Laurier | University of Saint-Louis - Brussels, Belgium |
| Michael Adams | Queensland University of Technology, Australia |
| Jean-Noël Colin | University of Namur, Belgium |
| Haris Mouratidis | University of Brighton, UK |
| Giovanni Meroni | Polytechnic University of Milan, Italy |

# Improving the Efficiency of a Blockchain-Based Confidential Registered e-Delivery Protocol

Macià Mut-Puigserver⬤, Rosa Pericàs-Gornals,
M. Magdalena Payeras-Capellà(✉)⬤, and Miquel À. Cabot-Nadal

Departament de Ciències Matemàtiques i Informàtica, Universitat de les Illes Balears,
07122 Palma, Spain
{macia.mut,rosa.pericas,mpayeras,miquel.cabot}@uib.cat

**Abstract.** Security protocols based on blockchain technology need to achieve some relevant features to spread their acceptance. In this paper we present a set of implementation techniques to enhance the efficiency and the operational cost of such protocols. We have recently presented a powerful protocol for confidential registered e-deliveries of data [2] that fulfills the security requirements for this service thanks to the use of blockchain technologies. However, the efficiency and the execution costs could reduce its viability. In this paper we present an improvement of this protocol acting in three different aspects of the protocol: the way the encrypted data is stored, now we use an off-chain storing scheme; the cryptosystem used, making it possible to use shorter keys with the same security level; and the implementation of the smart contracts, where more efficient functions are used allowing lower costs in the creation of the deliveries. The paper has a description of the protocol with the new improvements. Also we have implemented, tested and compared the new proposal with the original one, showing how the costs have been reduced significantly.

**Keywords:** Certified e-Delivery · Blockchain · Smart contract · Confidentiality · Efficiency

## 1 Introduction

Many applications require the delivery of data from one user to another. In a registered e-Delivery, the application must not only deliver the data but also provide pieces of evidence of the delivery of the data, that is, it must provide a non-repudiation of origin proof together with a non-repudiation of reception proof.

For this reason, registered e-Delivery services, together with other services, like electronic purchases and electronic signature of contracts, require the fair exchange of the items. A fair exchange aims to provide equal treatment to all the involved parties. At the end of a protocol execution, either each party has the

© The Author(s), under exclusive license to Springer Nature Switzerland AG 2022
J. Horkoff et al. (Eds.): CAiSE 2022, LNBIP 451, pp. 5–17, 2022.
https://doi.org/10.1007/978-3-031-07478-3_1

item it desires to obtain from the other involved party, or, if it is not the case, the exchange has not been performed successfully for any user, that is, any user has not received the desired element. In the case of registered e-Deliveries, a sender must deliver the data together with a non-repudiation of origin proof in exchange for a non-repudiation of reception proof from the receiver or set of receivers who can access the delivered data. Traditionally, almost all the proposals for registered e-Deliveries included a Trusted Third Party (TTP) to solve disputes and assure fairness between the different parties of the exchange.

Together with fairness, other ideal properties of the protocols are: effectiveness, timeliness, non-repudiation and transferability of evidence [1]. Recently, a few papers propose the use of blockchain to manage the registered e-Deliveries, taking advantage of the fact that blockchain is a technology that offers an immutable registry of data. Blockchain can be used to obtain fairness and can reduce or even remove the need for trusted third parties.

The protocol we presented in [2] achieves, at the same time, the best properties of previous solutions [3,4]. The protocol does not require the involvement of a TTP at any moment while it allows the e-Delivery of confidential data. In order to achieve confidentiality in an exchange that is publicly managed by a smart contract, the delivered data must be encrypted until the acceptance by the receiver, when the non-repudiation of reception proof is provided by the receiver. Moreover, the smart contract cannot access the key required to decrypt the delivered data, so the key cannot be included in clear in a transaction. The smart contract must assure that the receivers will be able to decrypt the data after acceptance of the delivery, and in multiparty scenarios, the smart contract must assure that all the receivers decrypt the same data.

Even though [2] achieves the desired properties, and the paper presents a performance analysis proving its viability, the efficiency of the system would be improved if the costs associated with the deployment and execution of the smart contracts could be reduced. In this paper we present how the costs can be reduced by acting in three different aspects of the protocol: the storage system for the encrypted data, the cryptographic algorithms used and the method used to create the smart contracts for each delivery. The resulting protocol maintains the desired properties of the original one since the steps of the fair exchange and the generated proofs are the same. We include in the paper the description of the improved protocol, the cost analysis and the comparison of the results with those of [2], proving how the execution costs have been reduced significantly.

## 2   Technologies Used in the Improvement of the Protocol

Our previous protocol, as it's explained in detail in [2], is based in the use of the Ethereum blockchain system, which thanks to the *Ethereum Virtual Machine* provides a distributed *Turing Complete* machine that makes use of the called *Smart Contracts* programs. And also thanks to the blockchain network's main features, it provides the protocol with the properties of immutability, fairness, transferability, accountability and non-repudiation of the data transferred over the network. Therefore, this improvement also uses the Ethereum blockchain network due to its main features, providing a scenario to compare the implementation of both protocols. Then, as it has been introduced in the previous section, we have changed the storage system for the encrypted data, replacing the on-chain storage of the encrypted registered e-Delivery content with the use of the decentralized storage system IPFS. Moreover, in order to be able to use shorter encryption keys to maintain the security level, we have changed the *ElGamal* cryptosystem algorithm for Elliptic Curve Cryptography (ECC). Finally, to obtain the best price rates on new e-Delivery smart contracts deployment, the new implementation uses the Factory Clone programming pattern. In this section, we briefly present these three new technologies.

## 2.1   IPFS

IPFS provides a distributed peer to peer system where users can store any type of content that will be shared with all the network users, getting a censorship-resistant system. The main difference with the HTTP protocol is that IPFS uses content addressing, unlike HTTP, which uses location addressing. The IPFS content addressing protocol identifies the content by a CID, a cryptographic hash of the content used as the content address. The users send it to the IPFS nodes to obtain the content. IPFS provides immutability of the stored content, for the simple fact that if a stored data is edited then its CID will change [5].

In the implementation of the improved protocol we have used the Infura IPFS gateway to perform the process of uploading and downloading a delivery. The Infura IPFS service also provides us the pinning of the documents until six months after the last access or document upload. The pinning service fixes permanently a CID content to a node so this content is excluded from being deleted by the garbage collector system [5] that periodically removes the not recently used content stored in a node, in order to clean part of the node memory [6]. In other words, the pinning service prevents certain content from being deleted completely from the network. In addition, a proprietary IPFS node could be used, then there would be no time limit for the pinned files and, to avoid possible losses, this node can join a group of nodes that also perform the pinning of the shared data, or even make use of a higher level service like Filecoin[1].

## 2.2   Elliptic Curve Cryptography (ECC)

The Elliptic Curve Cryptography (ECC) represents the approach to establishing public-key systems based on elliptic curves over finite fields. In comparison with cryptosystems based on modular exponentiation operations, the ECC can use significantly shorter parameters to achieve a fixed security level, which is a great advantage when they have to be stored on-chain [14].

Before executing the registered e-Delivery protocol, in order to configure the protocol operational conditions, the following ECC parameters must be published, ensuring privacy and security:

---

[1] https://filecoin.io.

- A finite field $F_p$ of $p$ elements, where $p$ is a prime number.
- The elliptic curve on $F_p$: $E(F_p)$.
- The cyclic subgroup generator of points over the selected elliptic curve with order $n$: $G$.
- The cofactor of the subgroup generated by $G$: $h$. It is generally less than 4, because is the same as the order of the elliptic curve divided by the order of the cyclic subgroup $n$.
- The product of the point $P$ on the elliptic curve and the scalar $b$: $P\mathrm{x}[b]$.
- A user secret key randomly generated: $a \leftarrow [1, n-1]$.
- A user public key: $A = G\mathrm{x}[a]$.
- The other users must verify that $A$ is a valid point of the curve and that $A\mathrm{x}[h]$ is not a point in the infinite.

### 2.3  Factory Clone Smart Contracts

The Factory Clone programming pattern is a better gas cost solution to the Factory method programming pattern, used in the original registered e-Delivery protocol implementation. The traditional factory method uses a Factory Contract that deploys new contracts and manages the new registered smart contracts, in our case, the registered e-Deliveries, achieving an easiest management system of the newly registered e-Deliveries and also a simple address storage method.

The *clones*, also known as *minimal proxies*, have the same objective as the traditional factory, but reducing the gas cost. The pattern is explained in the standard ERC1167 [7], which provides very simple functionality to clone a contract in an immutable way. The standard presents a minimal Solidity bytecode implementation that delegates all calls to a known and fixed address.

Using the implementation with clones, instead of deploying the e-Delivery smart contract each time a new e-Delivery is registered, we deploy a cheaper minimal e-Delivery contract that points to the e-Delivery smart contract that has been previously deployed on-chain. So, the minimal contracts delegate all calls to the implementation to this main smart contract that is used as a reference.

## 3  Improved Protocol

The improvement of the original Registered e-Delivery Protocol [2] presents the same phases of the original version, with some enhancements thanks to the new technologies introduced. There are three compulsory phases *Creation*, *Acceptation* and *Finalization*, and two optional phases, *Cancellation* and *Verification*.

However, prior to explaining each phase in detail, we describe how the protocol works in general terms. Alice, the e-Delivery sender, registers the delivery encrypted message, achieving the necessary confidentiality. Nevertheless, the smart contract will have to check that all receivers can decrypt the same delivered message. Before this verification, the receivers have to generate the called *Notification Keys* and accept the registered e-Delivery in the *Accept* phase. The

*Notification Keys* will be finally used by Alice when she executes the *Finish* phase, to encrypt the delivery message encryption key, allowing the user to obtain the e-Delivery content. The *Accept* and *Finalization* phases are restricted by two timelines defined by Alice. A first deadline, *term1*, sets the time before which the receivers can accept the e-Delivery. From this (*term1*) to the next deadline, (*term2*), Alice can finish the registered e-Delivery, sending the encryption key to the receivers that have accepted it. The verification made by the smart contract by means of a ZKP (Schnorr Zero-Knowledge Proof [10]) is performed on-chain, assuring that Alice provides the same e-Delivery content for all receivers, preserving, at the same time, the confidentiality of the exchanged message. Specifically, the ZKP doesn't allow the smart contract to obtain the e-Delivery content, however, it provides the tools to detect that the key to obtaining the decrypted message is the same for all receivers.

The phases of the original protocol have been modified as follows:

1. **Creation.** *Alice* generates her pair of public and private encryption keys $(a, A)$ and generates the random seed $v$ that will be used to encrypt the message $M$. If it is necessary, for this encryption operation, the content of the message can be divided into fragments ($M[j]$).

   Then, before the encryption, *Alice* generates the element $V$ of an adapted method of the Elliptic Curve Integrated Encryption Scheme (ECIES) [8,9]. Element $V$ is used as a commitment to the emission of the right key by *Alice*. It will be verified by the smart contract through the non-interactive Schnorr Zero-Knowledge Proof [10], used on the *Finish* phase to verify that all receivers have access to the same $v$, to decrypt the registered message.

---

**Subprotocol 1:** Step 1. Creation

---

1. *Alice* :
   Generation of $a \leftarrow [1, n-1]$, $A = Gx[a]$, $v \leftarrow [1, n-1]$, $M$
   $key = random.seed(hash(v))$
   Encryption of $M$.
       If required, fragmentation of $M$ in blocks: $M[j]$
       $V = Gx[v]$
       **FOR** $j = 1$ **TO** $M.length$
           $C[j] = M[j] \oplus key$
           $key = random.seed(hash(key))$
2. *Alice* ▶ IPFS: Upload C $= hashIPFS$
3. *Alice* ▶ $SM.creation(Alice, B, V, hashIPFS, A, term1, term2, D)$
4. *SM* :
   $State_i = Created, \forall i$

---

Following the encryption of the message, the improved implementation performs the upload of the encrypted message to the IPFS system, from which *Alice* obtains the content CID (i.e. IPFS identification label of a message) of the delivery. At this point, *Alice* executes the function *creation()*, where the Factory Clone smart contract clones a new Delivery smart contract, with all the parameters set. This function includes: the set of receiving B, *Alice* commitment $V$, the IPFS CID of the encrypted delivery $hashIPFS$ and two deadlines: $term1$ for each receiver to accept the delivery and $term2$ for $Alice$ to finish the exchange. Also, as an additional parameter, there is an optional payment for the service or a deposit $D$. Finally, the state is updated for each receiver $i$ and the Smart Contract defines the state as $Created$.

2. **Accept.** If a receiver decides to accept a registered e-Delivery, he has to do it before the deadline $term1$, by executing the corresponding function $accept()$ of the Delivery smart contract. Otherwise, a rejection of the receiver is assumed. In the $Accept$ phase, the receiver $Bob_i$, generates its own public and private shared notification keys $(b_i, B_i)$, which will be shared between a concrete recipient $(Bob_i)$ and the sender. To share the notification key that will be used in the $Finish$ phase on the ZKP step, first $Bob_i$ generates his encryption nonce $s_i$ and the challenge variable $c_i$. Next, he generates parameters $Z_{i_1}$, $Z_{i_2}$ to allow Alice to get the secret shared key $b_i$.

When $Bob_i$ has generated all the required parameters, he can execute the Smart Contract function $accept()$, sending $Z_{i_1}$, $Z_{i_2}$, $B_i$ and $c_i$ parameters, which are needed by Alice on the Finish phase to generate the response $(r_i)$ to the challenge $(c_i)$ sent by $Bob_i$ to $Alice$.

---

**Subprotocol 2:** Step 2. Accept

---

    1. $Bob_i$ :
        Generation of the parameters: $b_i \leftarrow [1, n-1], B_i = Gx[b_i], s_i$
        $Z_{i_1} = Gx[s_i], Z_{i_2} = (Ax[s_i]) \oplus (b_i), c_i \leftarrow [1, n-1]$
    2. $Bob_i$ ▶ $SM.accept(Z_{i_1}, Z_{i_2}, B_i, c_i)$
    3. SM:
        **IF**$(now < term_1)$ AND $(Id == B_i)$ AND $(State_i == Created)$
            $State_i = Accepted$
            Add $B_i$ to $B'$

---

3. **Finish.** Between the deadlines $(term1, term2)$, $Alice$ can finish the registered e-Delivery process executing the $finish()$ function for all $Bob_i$ that have accepted the notification, from now on $Bob'$ users.

First of all, in this phase, $Alice$ must create the response for each challenge received by $Bob'$ users, using the element $v$, used in the first phase of the protocol to encrypt the delivery, the secret shared notification key $(b_i)$ and $Bob_i$ challenge $(c_i)$. So, $Alice$ must obtain from the delivery smart contract $B_i$ public key, $Z_{i_1}$ and $Z_{i_2}$ parameters and the receiver challenge $c_i$. Using these parameters, $Alice$ decrypts the shared secret notification key $(b_i)$ and then encrypts the delivery encryption key $v$ using the challenge received and $Bob_i$ shared secret key. Finally, she invokes the $finish()$ function of the smart contract to submit the result.

Then, $Bob_i$ can request the parameters needed to the smart contract, getting the IPFS CID of the delivery $(hashIPFS)$, Alice's public key $A$ and Alice challenge response $r_i$. Then, $Bob_i$ needs to obtain the encrypted delivery, through an IPFS request sending the *hashIPFS* parameter. Once, $Bob_i$ has the encrypted delivery message $C$, using the received $r_i$, his $c_i$ and $b_i$ parameters only have to decrypt $C$ through an XOR function with the key derived from $v$.

---

**Subprotocol 3:** Step 3. Finish

---

1. *Alice* ▶ SM.getParameters(): $Z_{i_1}, Z_{i_2}, B_i, c_i$
2. *Alice* :
    Decrypts: $b_i = Z_{i_2} \oplus (Z_{i_1}x[a])$
    Generation of $r_i = v - b_i * c_{i\ modn}$
3. $A$ ▶ SM.finish($r_i$)
4. SM:
    **IF** $(Id == Alice)$ AND $((term_1 < now < term_2)$ OR $((Bob' == Bob)$
        AND $(now < term2)))$
        **FOR** $(\forall Bob_i \in Bob')$
            **IF** $V == Gx[r_i] + B_ix[c_i]$
                $State_i = Finished$
        **FOR** $(\forall Bob_i \notin Bob')$
            $State_i = Rejected$
        Deposit $D$ is refunded to *Alice*
5. $Bob_i$ ▶ SM.getParameters(): $hashIPFS, A, r_i$
6. $Bob_i$ ▶ IPFS: Download $hashIPFS = C$
7. $Bob_i$: $v = r_i + b_i * c_{i\ modn}$
    $key = random.seed(hash(v))$
    **FOR** $j = 1$ **TO** $n$
        $M[j] = C[j] \oplus key$
        $key = random.seed(hash(key))$

---

4. **Cancellation of Acceptance.** The protocol takes into account the possible case in which the sender does not finish the registered e-Delivery. Therefore, an optional subprotocol is provided that will be executed in case *Alice* does not provide the decryption key once a receiver has accepted the registered e-Delivery.
    A user $B_i$ is allowed to cancel if *term2* has been exceeded and the delivery status is *Accepted*. The smart contract will change the state of the delivery from *Accepted* to *Cancelled*.

---

**Subprotocol 4:** Cancellation of Acceptance

---

1. $B_i$ ▶ SM.cancel()
2. SM:
    **IF**$(now >= term2, Id == B_i$ AND $State_i == Accepted)$
        $State_i = Cancelled$

---

5. **Verification.** As on the original implementation, all variables and states stored on the smart contract are public, allowing any verification carried out by the sender *Alice*, any receiver $Bob_i$ of the delivery and, also, from any third party.

# 4   Implementation of the Protocol

The implementation of the improved protocol can be found in our Github repository[2]. It has been developed from the creation of the smart contracts *Factory Clone* and *eDelivery* that provide the methods explained in the previous section. The *eDelivery* smart contract is responsible for the execution of the ZKP using an Elliptic Curve Cryptography library that provides the arithmetic operations over elliptic curves to achieve the ZKP calculations. For this purpose, the smart contract implementation uses the Witnet Foundation Elliptic Curve Library [11]. The *Factory Clone* smart contract has the *clone()* method, which follows the Open Zeppelin library presented at [12].

The two smart contracts of the improved implementation contain the same functions as the two smart contracts of the original implementation. There are only some changes due to the cryptographic improvement (i.e. from *ElGamal* cryptosystem to ECC). An explanation of the Solidity code of the smart contract is omitted due to the space limitation of the paper. However, the full content of our implementation is available at the Github site previously specified.

Besides the Solidity smart contracts code, we have also implemented a front-end interface using JavaScript React that allows the execution of the protocol in a user-friendly mode. Moreover, any user can make use of this interface to upload and download the delivery encrypted messages to the IPFS system.

In addition to that, the user interface has to be able to encrypt and decrypt the delivered messages and to generate all the elliptic curve parameters. In order to compute the parameters, we use an elliptic curve Javascript library [13] configured with the same *secp256k1* curve as in the Solidity library.

# 5   Performance Analysis and Comparison

Once we have finished the improved implementation of the protocol, we have tested it together with the original protocol, in order to determine the efficiency improvement in terms of cost. In the test we have evaluated the methods of the smart contract that define the three compulsory phases *Creation*, *Acceptation* and *Finalization*. These functions are the ones that execute more instructions on-chain and they depend on the three new technologies introduced. The cost tests have been made using the Hardhat environment, specifically executed over the provided local blockchain node.

In order to obtain data to determine the improvements introduced by the use of the IPFS system, the cost tests of the original implementation have been carried out again to have results for both protocols with a different number of receivers and different lengths of the delivered messages.

The improved implementation, as it has been explained in previous sections, uses ECC. Specifically, we have selected the *secp256k1* curve. This change has improved significantly the encryption security of the implementation, compared

---

[2] https://github.com/secomuib/ConfidentialRegisteredEDeliveryProtocolImproved-IPFS-ECC.

to the security provided by the same key length of the cryptosystem *ElGamal*. In order to analyze and compare the costs of the two implementations we have selected the key lengths which provide the same security level, and performed the required experiments to obtain the costs. Following the NIST recommendations [14], we have selected the key of 3072 bits for *ElGamal*, that provides the same security level of keys of 256 bits in the ECC implementation. Therefore, with this change, we have highly reduced the key bits stored in the blockchain.

We have evaluated the gas cost of the functions for both the original and the improved protocol, taking into account the parameters that affect the cost.

- The *createDelivery()* function of the original protocol requires an amount of gas that depends on the message length. For this reason, we have tested it with three message lengths (10, 5000 and 10000 characters). In contrast, the message length doesn't affect the improved protocol, because it only stores on the blockchain the CID of IPFS that identifies the message.
- The *accept()* and *finish()* functions are independent of the message length, but *finish()* depends on the number of receivers.
- The *deploy()* function of the Factory Clone smart contract doesn't have significant changes from the original implementation and it is independent of the number of receivers and the message length. It costs 3,419,964 Gwei in both protocols.

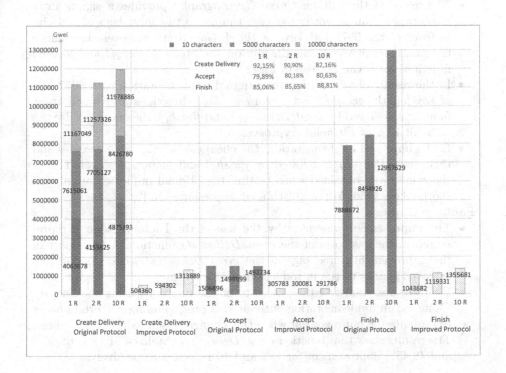

**Fig. 1.** Graphic of the results obtained in the functions tests.

Figure 1 shows the results of the analysis. The horizontal axis of the graph is divided in the three compulsory phases (*Create Delivery*, *Accept* and *Finish*). Each one of these parts is also divided into two sections, one for the *Original Protocol* and the other one for the *Improved Protocol*.

Sections are formed by three bars that represent the test results of a registered e-Delivery with 1, 2 and 10 receivers, (1R, 2R and 10R, respectively). Over each vertical bar, the cost results of the corresponding function test are indicated, computed in values of gas, setting a gas price of 1 gwei.

The first section of Fig. 1 represents the *Create Delivery* of the *Original Protocol*. In this section there are three bars that represent the gas cost for 1, 2 and 10 receivers. In addition, each bar also represents the results for the three message lengths, presented in the legend at the top of the graph.

Finally, in the center of the figure, we present the percentage cost reduction between the results of the *Improved Protocol* and the *Original Protocol* of the same method, providing a quantitative evaluation of the improvement. The percentage of improvement for the *Create Delivery* function has been computed from the average results of the three message lengths for each number of receivers.

From the results introduced in Fig. 1 we can determine how each improvement has affected the efficiency of the protocol.

– **Elliptic Curve Cryptography:**
   - The usage of the Elliptic Curve Cryptography provides a significantly important enhancement in gas cost thanks to the short keys of 256 bits in front of the 3072 bits keys of the *ElGamal* cryptosystem to achieve the same security level. Specifically on the *createDelivery()* and *finish()* functions, as it can be seen in Fig. 1.
   - In the results obtained from the original implementation with 3072 bits of key length, *accept()* and *factory deploy()* functions are the cheapest functions, followed by *createDelivery()* and *finish()*, the ones that use the 3072 bit keys of *ElGamal* cryptosystem.
   - In the improved implementation, the cheapest functions are *accept()* and then *createDelivery()*, followed by *finish()* and *factory deploy()*. This is the same order obtained when testing the original implementation with shorter keys (256, 512 or 1024), as it is presented in [2].
– **Factory Clone:**
   - The improvement generated by the use of the Factory Clone is represented in the gas costs of the *createDelivery()* function. A large part of the improvement percentage of the *createDelivery()* section in Fig. 1 is achieved thanks to the introduction of this feature.
   - We have also analyzed the gas costs of the functions using the Factory Clone vs. an implementation without this programming pattern in order to evaluate the improvement when this change is isolated from the others. The results show that function *createDelivery()* obtains a 71,78%, 68,36% and 49,45% improvement for 1, 2 and 10 receivers respectively.

– **Use of IPFS:**
  - The *createDelivery()* function has also obtained a cost reduction thanks to the use of the IPFS system to store encrypted registered e-delivery messages. As it is represented in the section *Create Delivery* of Fig. 1, this improvement increments with the number of characters used.
  - This feature enhances the implementation by providing an easy way to deliver not only text messages but to deliver any type of file and size.

When the three improvements are evaluated together, we have obtained a cost reduction between 79,89% and 92,15%, as it can be seen in the table that appears in Fig. 1. From this cost analysis we can state that we have maintained the most important properties of the registered e-Delivery system on the improved protocol, and we have significantly boosted the efficiency in terms of cost, related to the costs obtained in [2].

## 6   Conclusions

There are some important features that will help to introduce blockchain-based applications to the general public. We think that improving efficiency and costs are capital for such adoption. In this paper we present how we have improved a powerful blockchain-based security protocol for certified e-Delivery that originally was able to remove the need for trusted third parties while providing fairness, confidentiality and multiparty capabilities. Since the original protocol fulfilled the desired security properties we have focused our improvement on the efficiency and cost of the protocol, modifying the interactions among the actors of the protocol and also changing the cryptographic operations performed in some phases of the protocol. Concretely, we have changed the place where the encrypted data are stored, we have also changed the cryptosystem used to encrypt the data and we have used more efficient functions in the smart contracts.

With these improvements, we have achieved a solution where the encrypted data can be accessed off-chain. Moreover, the keys used in the new cryptosystem can be shorter while maintaining the same security level. We have described the new protocol and how we have implemented it. Later the original and the improved protocol have been compared. We have shown how the new protocol reduces significantly the cost associated with the deployment and execution of the smart contracts. We have presented the percentage of reduction for each function depending on the number of receivers. For all functions and number of receivers, the improved protocol presents a cost reduction higher than 80%. We can conclude that the presented protocol is secure and efficient, making it a perfect solution for the registered e-Delivery service. Thus, the patterns that are presented in this paper can be shown as a set of best implementation practices for security protocols deployment using blockchain technology.

In future work, we intend to do a more detailed study about the use of IPFS for encrypted data. Since, sharing publicly sensitive data could represent a vulnerable point in the system. Thus, for that reason, we will study the implementation using some alternative systems such as Smart Vault[3].

**Acknowledgments.** We acknowledge the Ministerio de Ciencia e Innovación (MCI), the Agencia Estatal de Investigación (AEI) and the European Regional Development Funds (ERDF) for their support to the project Fair Exchange, Loyalty and TIckets with blockCHAIN (FeltiCHAIN) RTI2018-097763-B-I00.

# References

1. Zhou, J., Deng, R., Bao, F.: Some remarks on a fair exchange protocol. In: Proceedings 3rd International Workshop Practice Theory Public Key Cryptography (PKC), vol. 1751, pp. 46–57, January 2000
2. Mut-Puigserver, M., Cabot-Nadal, M.A., Payeras-Capellà, M.M.: Removing the trusted third party in a confidential multiparty registered eDelivery protocol using blockchain. IEEE Access **8**, 106855–106871 (2020). https://doi.org/10.1109/ACCESS.2020.3000558
3. Payeras-Capellà, M.M., Mut-Puigserver, M., Cabot-Nadal, M.A.: Blockchain-based system for multiparty electronic registered delivery services. IEEE Access **7**, 95825–95843 (2019). https://doi.org/10.1109/ACCESS.2019.2929101
4. Payeras-Capellà, M.M., Mut-Puigserver, M., Cabot-Nadal, M.A.: Smart contract for multiparty fair certified notifications. In: 2018 Sixth International Symposium on Computing and Networking Workshops (CANDARW), pp. 459–465 (2018). https://doi.org/10.1109/CANDARW.2018.00089
5. Politou, E., Alepis, E., Patsakis, C., Casino, F., Alazab, M.: Delegated content erasure in IPFS. Future Gener. Comput. Syst. **112**, 956–964 (2020)
6. Guidi, B., Michienzi, A., Ricci, L.: Data persistence in decentralized social applications: the IPFS approach. In: 2021 IEEE 18th Annual Consumer Communications & Networking Conference (CCNC), pp. 1–4 (2021). https://doi.org/10.1109/CCNC49032.2021.9369473
7. Murray, P., Welch, N., Messerman, J.: EIP-1167: minimal proxy contract. Ethereum Improvement Proposals, no. 1167, June 2018. https://eips.ethereum.org/EIPS/eip-1167
8. ISO/IEC 18033–2, Information Technology - Security Techniques - Encryption Algorithms - Part 2: Asymmetric Ciphers, International Organization for Standardization/International Electrotechnical Commission (2006)
9. Gayoso Martínez, V., Hernández Álvarez, F., Hernández Encinas, L., Sánchez Ávila, C.: A comparison of the standardized versions of ECIES. In: 2010 Sixth International Conference on Information Assurance and Security, Atlanta, GA, pp. 1–4 (2010)
10. Hao, F.: Schnorr non-interactive zero-knowledge proof. RFC 8235, September 2017. https://tools.ietf.org/html/rfc8235
11. Witnet: "elliptic-curve-solidity", NPM Package. https://www.npmjs.com/package/elliptic-curve-solidity
12. OpenZeppelin Docs, "Proxies - Minimal Clones". https://docs.openzeppelin.com/contracts/4.x/api/proxy#Clones

---

[3] https://docs.lightstreams.network/products/smart-vault.

13. Fedor Indutny: Fast elliptic curve cryptography in plain javascript. NPM Package (2021). https://www.npmjs.com/package/elliptic
14. Barker, E., Barker, W., Burr, W., Polk, W., Smid, M.: Recommendation for Key Management Part 1: General (rev. 3). NIST Special Publication 800(57), pp. 1–147 (2012)

# Multi-authority Decentralized Attribute-Based Authorization Framework

Kimheng Sok[1]([✉])[ORCID], Jean Noël Colin[1][ORCID], and Kimtho Po[2]

[1] NaDI Research Institute, University of Namur, Namur, Belgium
kimheng.sok@student.unamur.be, jean-noel.colin@unamur.be
[2] Institute of Technology of Cambodia, Phnom Penh, Cambodia
pokimtho@itc.edu.kh

**Abstract.** The advancement in collaborative work among multiple institutions results in tremendous data sharing and, at the same time raises concerns about data security and privacy. Current systems are mostly built upon a centralized model, so the system requires one authority to concede another authority or mitigate trust to a trusted third party.

In this paper, we propose a multi-authority decentralized attribute-based authorization framework illustrated in an eHealth scenario that provides resilience and transparency, enforces data privacy, and allows each authority to enforce their access policy on the shared data. The framework operates on Blockchain technology and multi-authority attribute-based encryption. Our framework protects against malicious single authority who aims to grant permission to users to the shared data. Moreover, we optimize the user key structure that could reduce the key size of the key set by a factor of up to n! where n is the number of attributes in the user key to eliminate brute-force attacks. We implement the framework, show the system performance, and prove the efficiency of our proposed framework.

**Keywords:** Security · Privacy · Authorization framework · Blockchain · D-MA-ABE

## 1 Introduction

### 1.1 Motivation

The reason we choose eHealth as a scenario for proof of concept is that the health care sector is a multi-authority industry that includes: hospitals, laboratories, radiologists, pharmacies, patients, insurance companies, financial institutions, government agencies, research institutions, partners, other referral health care providers, donors, suppliers, auditors, and regulators. Health care data is one of the valuable and sensitive assets to be protected. That is why health care providers are required to comply with certain regulations depending on

© The Author(s), under exclusive license to Springer Nature Switzerland AG 2022
J. Horkoff et al. (Eds.): CAiSE 2022, LNBIP 451, pp. 18–30, 2022.
https://doi.org/10.1007/978-3-031-07478-3_2

their regions such as Health Insurance Portability and Accountability Act 1996 (HIPAA) [1], General Data Protection Regulation 25 May 2018 (GDPR) [2].

Most of the designs of the system so far are using a centralized governance approach to manipulate access to data. There is a central authority that creates user accounts, sets user roles, and manages access policy by granting access rights to each user, resulting in some drawbacks such as centralized decision making and management overhead. Moreover, due to the centralized nature of the system, it is subject to a single point of failure. Therefore, we aims to build a system in a decentralized way to answer the problems above by using Blockchain technology [3]. Blockchain technology provides many benefits, firstly, it maintains the integrity of the data due to its immutable feature. Secondly, historical data inside the Blockchain could also be served as an audit log. Thirdly, Blockchain allows multi-party to join the network for collaborative work and data sharing. Lastly, a smart contract that deploys inside Blockchain nodes could serve as access control. In addition, we also use encryption techniques to preserve data privacy.

## 1.2   Our Contributions

In this paper, we propose a multi-authority decentralized attribute-based authorization framework. The main contributions of this paper are summarized as follows:

1. **Design multi-authority decentralized access control architecture**, which allows multi-authority to set a joint access policy on the shared data.
2. **Propose decentralized multi-authority attribute-based encryption (D-MA-ABE) algorithms** for privacy enforcement and protection.
3. **Optimize user key structure** to reduce the brute-force attack vector.
4. **Implement the proposed framework** for proof of concept and performance evaluation.

## 1.3   Paper Organization

The rest of the paper is organized as follows: Sect. 2 presents background information; Sect. 3 provides an overview of related work; Sect. 4 shows our approach, and overall architecture; Sect. 5 demonstrates our implementation and performance evaluation; finally, Sect. 6 deliberate the conclusion and future works.

# 2    Background Information

## 2.1    Notations

| Symbols | Description | Symbols | Description |
|---------|-------------|---------|-------------|
| AA | Attribute Authority | $Uattr$ | User attributes |
| DO | Data Owner | $UK_i$ | User sub key from $AA_i$ |
| DU | Data User | $UK$ | User Key |
| CSP | Cloud Service Provider | $PKs$ | All public key of AAs |
| $\lambda$ | Security Parameter | $K$ | AES Key |
| $PP$ | Public Parameter | $AP$ | Access Policy |
| $SK_i$ | Secret Key of authority i | $M$ | Message |
| $PK_i$ | Public Key of authority i | $CK$ | Cipher Key |
| $Uid$ | User identity | $CT$ | Cipher Text |

There are four main actors in the system:

**AA (Attribute Authority):** An AA is in charge of issuing a user subkey that contains certain attributes for data users (DU).

**DO (Data Owner):** A DO is an entity that owns and controls the data to be shared. A DO specifies access control policies for the data it shares, there could be multiple DOs in our system. A DO could also be an AA, but AA is not necessary to be a DO.

**DU (Data User):** A DU is an entity that wants to access the data shared by DOs.

**CSP (Cloud Service Provider):** A CSP is an entity that hosts the encrypted files of DOs.

In order to understand how we design our system; we need to have a basic understanding of Attribute-based encryption and Blockchain technology.

## 2.2    Attribute-Based Encryption

There are several types of attribute-based encryption (ABE) systems, one is Key-Policy (KP-ABE) [12,13], and another one is Ciphertext-Policy (CP-ABE) [14]. For example, we encrypt a message with an access policy *"user.role = doctor and user.org = hospital1 and user.group = emergency_staff"*, so the user needs to request a user key from their attribute authority. In this case, the hospital if their user key contains the attributes *{hospital1, doctor, emergency_staff}*, user can access the data, otherwise not. Most ABE scheme relies on a centralized approach of using Key Generation Center (KGC), while others rely on a decentralized approach such as multi-attribute authorities ciphertext-policy attribute-based encryption (MAA-CP-ABE) [15]. Our attribute-based encryption scheme is extended from the work in [15]; we will discuss the extension of the algorithm in Sect. 4.2. Our encryption scheme is applied in a decentralized way called by the user application and smart contracts in the Blockchain network, we called it Decentralized Multi-Authority Attribute-Based Encryption (D-MA-ABE).

## 2.3 Blockchain and Smart Contract

Blockchain [3] is a peer-to-peer distributed ledger technology that has immutability, transparency, and distributed property which could be used to ensure the integrity and availability of the system. Smart contract [4] is a computerized transaction protocol that executes the terms of a contract; it is the computer programs business logic that executes when the condition is verified, and it can be used to set an agreement between multi-authority for access control privilege without a trusted third party in the middle. To understand more about Blockchain technology opportunities and challenges please refer to [16]. There are different types of Blockchain. Public Blockchain where everyone is allowed to join the network, private Blockchain which only authorized members are allowed to join. We choose Hyperledger Fabric [7], as it is a private Blockchain, which some people consider as a consortium Blockchain. It is built for the enterprise by design that allows multiple enterprises to work together as a consortium. We also choose the attribute-based access control (ABAC) model suitable for defining a fine-grained access policy as well as the complex access control rules [17].

## 3  Related Work

Blockchain technology has become popular; the use of smart contracts as an access control has gained more attention from research communities. There are several papers targeting the same use case for secure data sharing [5,6] both papers are using Hyperledger Blockchain [7] with the eHealth use case. The idea in [5] is to create a Medichain that acts as another trusted third party storage and policy enforcement service between patient, caregiver, and medical clinic by granting full control to the patient, who is the data owner. It is a patient-centric health system that allows patients to be the owner of data and set access policies to their own data. If the patient is unable to perform the task by him/herself, the patient can designate the role to the caregiver to become the data owner. [6] is also using Hyperledger Blockchain together with the edge node for storage. Hyperledger access control list is used to verify the user identity, and attribute-based access control (ABAC) is used to enforce data on the edge node. The patient is the data owner who sets the policy on their data, and the doctor is a data user who requests to read the data. Both papers were using Hyperledger composer to create an access control policy that was already deprecated and declared the end of life in August 2021 by the Hyperledger community. None of the maintainers are actively developing new features. None of the maintainers are actively providing support via GitHub issues. In [8,9], both papers use Ethereum Blockchain [10] and attribute-based access control

(ABAC) for policy enforcement, but they have distinct approaches for creating their access control model; in [8] was built on the eXtensible Access Control Markup Language (XACML) Components that operate together with Ethereum smart contract. Most of the research works focus only on a single data owner to protect the confidentiality of their own data, but there have not been many works on multiple data owners controlling the shared data. On the other hand, [9] there is a concept of multi-authority whose roles are to attest the attributes from data users then provide attribute tokens back. Enough attribute tokens could be utilized to exchange for the encryption key, which is used to decrypt the requested data stored in the shared database. This paper also uses ciphertext-policy attribute-based encryption (CP-ABE) [11] to encrypt the data.

Table 1 shows the comparison between our framework we named it DRACO, and the other related work. We can notice there are different kinds of Blockchains such as Hyperledger [7] and Ethereum [10] that have been used to create authorization frameworks. Real data or encrypted data is usually stored off-chain, in edge node, private resource server (Private RS), share database (share DB), or outsourced to a cloud service provider (CSP). ABAC is the most well-known access control model to be used. Some works did not focus on encryption at rest, while some used different kinds of attribute-based encryption schemes for data encryption such as CP-ABE. In most of the works, there is only a single attribute authority (AA), while the use of multi-authority has grown in attention due to the increasing amount of collaborative work. None of the related work has ever optimized the user key structure.

**Table 1.** Related work comparison.

| Paper | Blockchain | Storage | AC model | Encryption | AA | Optimize UK |
|---|---|---|---|---|---|---|
| [5] | Hyperledger | Off-chain | DAC | YES | Single | NO |
| [6] | Hyperledger | Edge node | ABAC | NO | Single | NO |
| [8] | Ethereum | Private RS | ABAC | NO | Single | NO |
| [9] | Ethereum | Share DB | ABAC | CP-ABE | Multiple | NO |
| DRACO | Hyperledger | CSP | ABAC | D-MA-ABE | Multiple | YES |

## 4  Our Approach

### 4.1  Scenario

In order to understand the process of a decentralized authorization framework in a multi-authority environment, let us converge toward an eHealth scenario. The scenario begins when a patient is seeking health care services, with a doctor, who is an employee inside the hospital, and the insurer, who needs to access the billing information of the patient in order to reimburse the insurance fee in which the patient has subscribed. In this simple scenario, there are two big institutions: the hospital and the insurance company, which act as an attribute authority (AA) in our system to provide necessary attributes to their employees. In the patient-centric system, a patient is considered a data owner (DO), and at the same time an attribute authority (AA) too. In the hybrid system there could be multiple data owners as such both the health care institution and the patient are data owners (DOs), who can enforce their personal preference of the access policy on the patient records. Insurance companies might assign their employee to access patient's billing record so their employee acts as data user (DU) in the system that requests to read the billing information. As information is encrypted using D-MA-ABE, the data user (DU) needs to request all the subkeys from the correspondent attribute authorities to access the information of the patient. The business process could be extended to have multiple roles in each organization, with more than two organizations wishing to join the system.

## 4.2    System Architecture

Our authorization framework composes of five main components: Client Application, Blockchain network, D-MA-ABE Module (Crypt Module), Smart contracts, and Storage as shown in Fig. 1. All users in the system such as AA, DO, DU use client applications to communicate with the Blockchain network. First, they need to create an account in the Blockchain to establish the relationship between them. Once they are in a relationship, DU can request user subkeys from AA and use them to request data by calling the smart contract (chaincode) in the Blockchain network. To enforce and protect data privacy, users need to follow the D-MA-ABE protocol, so the D-MA-ABE module (Crypt Module) is implemented and embedded in the client applications and also inside each network peer. Due to the length of the paper, we will only discuss two main components here, which are the smart contract and the D-MA-ABE Module.

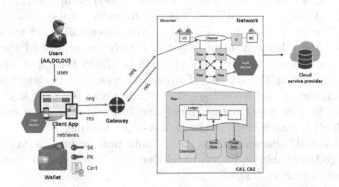

**Fig. 1.** Multi-authority decentralized authorization framework architecture.

**Smart Contract.** In Hyperledger Blockchain, a smart contract is also called chaincode, which is the program running on the Blockchain network. In Fig. 1

we illustrate four peers in which the smart contracts are installed, instantiated, and run. We create three smart contracts called AdminCC, AuthzCC, CryptCC. AdminCC is responsible for administrative tasks such as account creation, relationship establishment (ex. care circle, employment), system initialization, and setup phase. AuthzCC is responsible for authorization tasks such as key generation, merging user subkeys, and decryption phase, while CryptoCC is responsible for data encryption. The way we design smart contracts is for software modularity and separation of functionality and data sensitivity. The interaction of smart contracts could be found in Fig. 2.

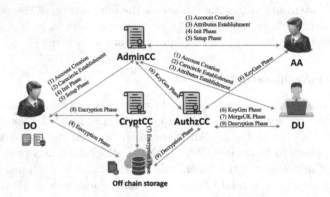

**Fig. 2.** Smart contracts architecture.

**D-MA-ABE Module.** decentralized multi-authority attribute-based encryption scheme (D-MA-ABE) follows the construction from the MAA-CP-ABE scheme [15] which consists of five main phases: GlobalSetup, AuthSetup, KeyGen, Encrypt, Decrypt. The scheme was not intended to use with Blockchain Technology. Therefore, in order to adapt to the decentralization workflow, we have extended the scheme in many aspects. Firstly, we separated the KeyGen phase into two different phases. Secondly, we modified the input and output of some algorithms in the scheme, Thirdly, we modified the encryption and decryption scheme so that we will get the constant size of cipher key. Fourthly, we optimized the user key structure. Lastly, we implemented smart contracts to interact with all the algorithms in the D-MA-ABE module.

Our D-MA-ABE scheme consists of six main phases: Init, Setup, Key Generation, Merge User subkeys, Encrypt and Decrypt. The details of the six-phase will be described in Sect. 5.1.

# 5  Implementation

## 5.1  D-MA-ABE Algorithms

Below are the D-MA-ABE six phases algorithms:

Suppose that we have a set of multi-authority $A = \{AA_i,\ AA_j\ ...,\ AA_n\}$, a message $M$ is the shared data that all attribute authorities want to set access policy on. $P_i$ is the policy of $AA_i$ on message $M$ and $P_j$ is the policy of $AA_j$ on message $M$. $AP = \{P_i,\ P_j,\ ...,\ P_n\}$ is the access policy set of all attributes authorities.

**i/Init:**

$$Init(\lambda) : PP \tag{1}$$

Init algorithm takes a security parameter $(\lambda)$ which is the size of the order in bits and outputs Public Parameter $(PP)$. One of the attribute authorities is called the init function and broadcasts output to all the relevant attribute authorities.

**ii/Setup:**

$$Setup(PP, i, \alpha, y) : SK_i, PK_i \tag{2}$$

Each time a new authority is introduced, setup will generate a random number $\alpha$ and $y$ to create the secret key $(SK)$ then produce the corresponding public key $(PK)$ which also includes the authority $(AA_i)$ with identity $(i)$ in it, so that we can verify the public key belongs to which authority. Then, each authority can generate a subkey embedding relevant user attributes.

**iii/KeyGen_i:**

$$KeyGen\_i(PP, SK_i, Uid, Uattr_i, r\_arr) : UK_i \tag{3}$$

The KeyGen stands for key generation, which is an algorithm that takes a Public Parameter $(PP)$, the Secret Key $(SK_i)$ of a particular authority $(AA_i)$, User identity $(Uid)$ that want to access information, user attributes $(Uattr_i)$ that attribute authority provides to the user and a random seed for cryptographic uses $(r\_arr)$ and output the User subkey $(UK_i)$. Users that want to access the restricted data need to request a User Key from the attribute authority. In case there is a multi-authority enforced access control policy on the shared data, the user needs to request a user subkey $(UK_i)$ from each attribute authority.

**iv/Merge_UK:**

$$Merge\_UK(\{UK_i, UK_j, ..., UK_n\}) : UK \tag{4}$$

Merge_UK is a function that takes all the user subkeys from each authority which belongs to the user and merges them together to generate a single user key $(UK)$. Each user subkey $UK_x$ where $x = \{i, j, ..., n\}$ is in the form of: $UK_x$ ={'GID':gid, 'keys':{attr1:{'K':'val', 'KP':'val'}, attr2:{'K':'val', 'KP':'val'}} each $UK_x$ contains user identity $gid$ and multiple attributes in random order $attr1, attr2$ with their respective cryptographic value $K$ and $KP$. Once merge together the final user key also contains multiple attributes from all the attribute authorities in random order as well. All possible positions of each attribute inside the user key creates a valid key set by a factor of n! where n is the number of attributes inside the user key. We optimize user key structure by sorting all key attributes in alphabetic order, so only a single key is valid during key validation. By doing so, we reduce the key size of the key set by a factor of n!.

## v/Encrypt:

$$Enc(PP, PKs, K, AP, M, s, w, tx\_r\_arr, path) : CK, CT \qquad (5)$$

Encrypt is an algorithm that encrypts messages $(M)$ with access policy $(AP)$ where $AP = \{P_i, P_j, ..., P_n\}$ and produces ciphertext $(CT)$. In theory, we want to encrypt $(M)$ the sensitive data such as patient personal information, patient health information, or financial information with the access policy $(AP)$ we want to enforce on that data. But in practice, encrypting the real data with access policy from different organizations consume a lot of processing time and storage depending on the size of the message, for this reason, we divide our encrypt algorithm into two steps, step one we use symmetry key $(K)$ which is used to encrypt the message $(M)$ to produce ciphertext $(CT)$, Ciphertext will be store off-chain mentioned by the variable $(path)$. Then, step two we encrypted the key $(K)$ with a multi-authority attribute-based encryption scheme with an access policy $(AP)$ of multi-authority so that our encrypt algorithm always take a constant time as the size of the key to be encrypted is always the same. To encrypt the key $(K)$ we need the public parameter $(PP)$, an access policy $(AP)$, the public key of all authority $(PKs)$, the symmetry key $(K)$ that we want to encrypt, $(s)$ secret share, $(w)$ zero share, and some random seed will be used for the cryptographic purpose $(tx\_r\_arr)$ and output the Cipher Key $(CK)$ that we store on the blockchain.

## vi/Decrypt:

$$Dec(PP, UK, CK, CT) : K, M \qquad (6)$$

Decrypt is an algorithm that decrypts $(CT)$ to get the message $(M)$. We also divide our Decrypt algorithm into two steps. Step one the algorithm decrypts the cipher key $(CK)$ by using the public parameter $(PP)$ and the user key $(UK)$ to obtain key $(K)$, and then step two it uses the key $(K)$ to decrypt cipher text $(CT)$ that retrieved from the off-chain storage to get the real message $(M)$.

## 5.2   Evaluation

In this section, we want to evaluate the strength of the algorithm with the threat model that we will define next; we prove that the system is preserving the security and privacy of information in the smart health system, and show the strength of the system in keeping malicious users away from revealing the secret data, let us see some attack scenarios below:

### Threat Model

**i. Honest-But-Curious Cloud Storage Provider.** When we upload data (patient health records) or other sensitive information in the cloud, we might trust our cloud storage provider but they might be honest-but-curious to see, share, or sell our data without our consent. These issues could be solved by encrypted data at rest with our decentralized multi-authority attribute-based encryption. Thus, the data has been encrypted before being sent to the storage; without a user key from multi-authority, no one could be able to decrypt the data and view it.

**ii. Malicious Single Authority.** Single attribute authority could maliciously generate a user sub key for any unauthorized user. In this case, the shared data is protected by the joint-access policy. Malicious authority could only generate the key which contains attributes that he/she is responsible for but not the attributes that belong to other authorities.

**iii. Malicious Attacker Wants to Modify Access Policy.** To decrypt the message, we need to have a user key with enough attributes or modify the policy, so that the enforcement is not too restricted. In that case, the malicious attacker could not do it because the hash of the encrypted message and the cipher key is stored in the Blockchain for transparency. Modifying encrypted messages or access policy will result in invalidating the hash value stored in the Blockchain ledger that maintains the integrity of the data, which is enforced by the consensus algorithm during the validating process.

**iv. User Key Collision.** Inside the user key, there is a list of attributes. Attributes in the user key are used as the decryption criteria. The position of those attributes could be in any random order. In our system, we optimize user key structure by sorting all the attributes before generating the final user key. This technique has never been done so far in any works that we have read. Why it is important to sort those attributes? Because if we did not there might be multiple valid user keys which increases the valid key set that provides a bigger chance for the attacker to compromise the user key.

## 5.3   Performance

In this section, we want to measure and evaluate the speed of the algorithm in two different cases. The first case runs the algorithm in a centralized model without using Blockchain, and the second case uses Hyperledger Blockchain. To measure the performance of our implementation, we used a laptop with Intel(R) Core(TM) i7-7700HQ CPU @ 2.80 GHz and 16.0 GB RAM. We run Hyperledger fabric stable version 1.4 first network as docker containers in virtual machines with Ubuntu operating system version 18.04, with pythons version 3.6 and a standard SS512 pairing group for attribute-based encryption. We show the comparison of the computing time without and with using a Hyperledger Blockchain network.

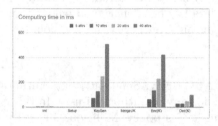

**Fig. 3.** Computing time without Blockchain.

Figure 3 shows the computing time in milliseconds of the six algorithms without using the Blockchain network. Init, setup, and merge user sub key algorithms take only 2 to 5 ms, while key generation, encryption, and decryption algorithms take exponential time depending on the number of attributes used. We show the computing time using 5, 10, 20, and 40 attributes.

| Time(ms) | PP | Setup | Keygen | MergeUK | Enc | Dec |
|---|---|---|---|---|---|---|
| Without Blockchain | 5 | 2 | 73 | 0 | 64 | 29 |
| With Blockchain | 5155 | 4817 | 4418 | 4671 | 5906 | 4842 |

*Blockchain (hyperledger fabric)*

**Fig. 4.** Computing time using blockchain.

Figure 4 shows that for all the six algorithms it takes approximately 4 to 5 s in addition to running on Hyperledger Blockchain. This additional computing cost is spent on the communication between peers in the Blockchain network. It is the cost that we need to pay for security such as system availability, data integrity, transparency, traceability, and multi-authority system.

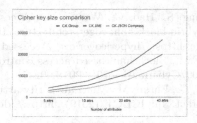

**Fig. 5.** Cipher key size comparison.

Cipher Key ($CK$) could be stored using different types of formats as shown in Fig. 5. The JSON compressed version consumes less memory than the pairing group operation; and the JSON Web Encryption (JWE) consumes higher memory.

## 6 Conclusion

In this paper, we presented a decentralized multi-authority attribute-based encryption framework and built a prototype, and implemented our D-MA-ABE algorithm and wrote three smart contracts AdminCC, AuthzCC, CryptCC for administration, authorization, and for data encryption, respectively. By using Blockchain technology and smart contract, we can eliminate central authority from the system, and enable multi-authority to work collaboratively. The integrity of data is maintained by the Blockchain consensus algorithm. Distributed ledger serves as the source of truth for transparency and audit. We also presented the threat models and performance of our framework. Our framework allows multi-authority to have equal control over the shared data, which is absent in many current systems. We have optimized the user key structure to protect against brute-force attacks which have never been done before. For our future work, we want to reduce network communication costs by performing operations in a localized way. All the source code will be available in our Github repository https://github.com/KimhengSOK. We also explore the possibilities of using Self-Sovereign Identity to present claims which involve additional stakeholders. Thanks to ARES, UNAMUR, and ITC for support.

## References

1. Health Insurance Portability and Accoutnability Act HIPAA. https://www.hhs.gov/hipaa/index.html. Accessed 7 Sept 2021
2. General Data Protection Regulation. https://www.gdpr.eu. Accessed 7 Sept 2021
3. Nakamoto, S.: Bitcoin: a peer-to-peer electronic cash system (2008)
4. Szabo, N.: The idea of smart contracts (1994)
5. Adam, S., Sara, R., Luke, B.: MediChain: a secure decentralized medical data asset management system. IEEE (2018). https://doi.org/10.1109/Cybermatics_2018.2018.00258

6. Mark, N., Chien-Chung, S., Hao, G., Wanxin, L.: Access control for electronic health records with hybrid blockchain edge architecture. IEEE (2019)
7. Hyperledger homepage. https://hyperledger.org. Accessed 7 Sept 2021
8. Aura, R., Damiano, P.M.: Blockchain based access control service. IEEE (2018). https://doi.org/10.1109/Cybermatics_2018.2018.00237
9. Chien-Chung, S., Hao, G., Ehsan, M.: Multi-authority attribute-based access control with smart contract. In: ICBCT (2019). https://doi.org/10.1145/3320154.3320164
10. Ethereum homepage. https://ethereum.org. Accessed 7 Sept 2021
11. Zhang, Y., Zheng, D., Chen, X., Li, J., Li, H.: Computationally efficient ciphertext-policy attribute-based encryption with constant-size ciphertexts. In: Chow, S.S.M., Liu, J.K., Hui, L.C.K., Yiu, S.M. (eds.) ProvSec 2014. LNCS, vol. 8782, pp. 259–273. Springer, Cham (2014). https://doi.org/10.1007/978-3-319-12475-9_18
12. Sahai, A., Waters, B.: Fuzzy identity-based encryption. In: Cramer, R. (ed.) EUROCRYPT 2005. LNCS, vol. 3494, pp. 457–473. Springer, Heidelberg (2005). https://doi.org/10.1007/11426639_27
13. Waters, B., Sahai, A.: Attribute based encryption for fine-grained access control of encrypted data. ACM (2006)
14. Bethencourt, J., Sabai, A., Waters, B.: Ciphertext-policy attribute-based encryption. IEEE (2007)
15. Water, B., Rouselakis, Y.: Efficient statically-secure large-universe multi-authority attribute-based encryption, pp. 315–332 (2015)
16. Sok, K., Colin, J.N., Po, K.: Blockchain and internet of things opportunity and challenges, pp. 150–154. ACM (2018). https://doi.org/10.1145/3287921.3287933
17. Colin, J.N., Laurent, E.: A flexible and centralized approach for access control in heterogeneous IoT environment (2019). https://doi.org/10.4018/IJHIoT.2019010102

# ISESL 2022

# Second International Workshop
# on Information Systems Engineering
# for Smarter Life (ISESL 2022)

## Preface

In the era of digitalization, new technologies (Internet of Things, augmented reality, cyber-physical systems, cloud computing, machine learning, and so on) change not only the functioning of enterprises and organizations, but also many aspects of human life: robots assisting disabled people, smart buildings providing security surveillance, digitally enhanced visits for museums, serious games for learning... the list is long. These various technologies are intended to improve or enhance the life of humans. In one way or another, they contribute to a smarter life.

Until now, digital technologies have been brought into the game as silo solutions. Reasoning holistically about information in the context of a bank or a manufacturing plant is routine practice. However, this approach is less common with emerging technologies for everyday life such as public digital applications where citizens are the central actors. Therefore, we deeply believe that methods, models, and techniques inherited from information systems engineering research could considerably improve the way humans interact with the digital world and would change the user experience. The perspective of information systems engineering research in the diverse setting of all kinds of smart life applications is united in this new research domain, which we coin smart life engineering.

The goal of the workshop is to bring together researchers and practitioners who are interested in the application of disruptive technologies to smarter life. The workshop topics include, but are not limited to, the application and emerging concepts of rising digital technologies to different fields of life through the perspective of information systems: artificial sentience and artificial intelligence, machine consciousness, cognitive spaces, patient experience design and health, point-of-care diagnosis, e-health, digital heritage, sustainable development, responsible ICT, digital education and teaching experience design for a worldwide audience, smart homes, smart buildings, smart roads, smart cities, cyberwarfare, digitalization in law enforcement, and ethical and philosophical aspects of new technology usage with humans. For this second edition, our ambition was to foster the emergence of the smart life research community. Round tables were organized during this workshop to discuss different issues related to smart life themes: smart technologies, smart systems, smart applications, and smart artefacts. Our primary aim is to create an IFIP working group that will serve as a community to execute the research agenda of smart life engineering.

For this second edition of the ISESL workshop, we selected six contributions (five full papers and one short paper) with a very nice variety of smart life engineering research. The first paper presents a review of smart city development methodologies and modeling languages. The second paper formalizes smart home activities based on sensor data using ontologies. The third paper presents an acceptance model of private electric vehicle charging infrastructure. The fourth paper suggests a sustainability matrix for smartphone applications. The fifth paper describes how habits could be formalized based on sensor data. The last paper gives insights into robots' artificial sentience through the analysis of a choreography.

We thank all authors of the submitted papers for their contribution to the ISESL 2022 workshop. We are grateful to all Program Committee members and the organizers of the CAiSE 2022 conference for their trust and support.

April 2022                                                              Elena Kornyshova
                                                                  Eric Gressier Soudan
                                                                           John Murray
                                                                     Sjaak Brinkkemper
                                                                    Rébecca Deneckère

# Organization

## Workshop Organizers

Elena Kornyshova      Conservatoire National des Arts et Métiers, France

Eric Gressier Soudan      Conservatoire National des Arts et Métiers, France

John Murray      San José State University, USA

Sjaak Brinkkemper      Utrecht University, The Netherlands

Rébecca Deneckère      University of Paris 1 Panthéon-Sorbonne, France

## Program Committee

Said Assar      Institut Mines-Telecom Business School, France

Isabelle Astic      Conservatoire National des Arts et Métiers, France

Judith Barrios Albornoz      University of Los Andes, Venezuela

Sjaak Brinkkemper      Utrecht University, The Netherlands

Sophie Chabridon      Télécom SudParis and, CNRS, France

Antonio Chella      Università di Palermo, Italy

Raja Chiky      Institut Supérieur d'Electronique de Paris, France

Rébecca Deneckère      University of Paris 1 Panthéon-Sorbonne, France

Eric Gressier Soudan      Conservatoire National des Arts et Métiers, France

Elena Kornyshova      Conservatoire National des Arts et Métiers, France

Sylvain Lefebvre      Toyota, Japan

José Machado      University of Minho, Portugal

Elisabeth Métais      Conservatoire National des Arts et Métiers, France

John Murray      San José State University, USA

Oscar Pastor      Universidad Politécnica de Valencia, Spain

Jolita Ralyté      University of Geneva, Switzerland

Mohammed Sellami      Institut Mines-Telecom Business School, France

| | |
|---|---|
| Samira Si-Said Cherfi | Conservatoire National des Arts et Métiers, France |
| Monique Snoeck | Katholieke Universiteit Leuven, Belgium |
| Carolyn Talcott | Stanford Research Institute International, USA |
| Robin Zebrowski | Beloit College, USA |
| Sergey Zykov | Higher School of Economics, Russia |

# Smart City Software: A Review of Development Methodologies and Modelling Languages

Anthony Simonofski[1]([✉]) [iD], Daria Sokolvak[2], and Estefanía Serral[2] [iD]

[1] University of Namur, Rue de Bruxelles 61, 5000 Namur, Belgium
anthony.simonofski@unamur.be
[2] KU Leuven, Oude Markt 13, 3000 Leuven, Belgium

**Abstract.** Smart cities aim to improve citizens' quality of life using technology. Due to their size, smart city projects often rely on dedicated software that is built using development methodologies and modelling languages. This paper aims at discovering what software development methodologies and modelling languages are being used in a Smart City context as well as revealing the drivers behind these choices. To do so, a literature review and six semi-structured interviews with practitioners in Belgian smart cities were conducted. The results demonstrate that there are various software development methodologies (Waterfall Model, Agile, Scrum, AUP, Hybrid Agile Methodology) and modelling languages (UML, SysML, BPMN, DSML, informal modelling) applied in a smart city context. This paper contributes to the understanding of the current state of software development methodologies and modelling languages within the smart city context. Moreover, by taking a closer focus on Belgian Smart Cities, it sheds light on the concrete state of practice and highlights the drivers and challenges associated with each approach.

**Keywords:** Smart city · Software · Modelling language · Software development

## 1 Introduction

During the last few years, we have observed an escalating tendency of a substantial number of people shifting towards living in the urban areas (Caragliu et al. 2011; Gaur et al. 2015). This growing number of city residents pushes city authorities to find ways for sustainable management of the increasing amount of organizational, technical, physical, and social concerns that emerge due to the high concentration of people. Rapid urbanization brings major challenges to the administration and general infrastructure of the city. These are a deficit of resources, falling into decay infrastructure, price fluctuations and scarcity of energy, troubles with human health, global environmental issues, and demand for improvement of economic potential (Nam and Pardo 2014). Despite this, Smart City projects can improve these challenges and create economic opportunities and social advantages for citizens.

J. Horkoff et al. (Eds.): CAiSE 2022, LNBIP 451, pp. 37–48, 2022.
https://doi.org/10.1007/978-3-031-07478-3_3

There is no unified and standard definition of a Smart City. Common for any Smart City remains the aim to deliver effective services to people, regulate and improve infrastructure, foster cooperation of economic stakeholders to promote progressive and innovative solutions in private and public sectors (Albino et al. 2015). The following objectives are being obtained via the deployment of two vital elements that fuel Smart City: Information Technology (IT) and human capital (Ahvenniemi et al. 2017; Hollands 2008). Smart Cities are complex systems composed of tons of digitalized and interconnected operations and ecosystems. This complexity requires a Smart City system to be designed, managed, and governed properly. In the heart of the Smart City, there are numerous devices and sensors that are being interconnected via high-speed network and together they form the Internet of Things (IoT) and generate an enormous amount of valuable data (Gaur et al. 2015). Data, consequently, boosts the creation of modern services for citizens, companies, and public administrations (Zanella et al. 2014). To properly configure, manage, and monitor IoT devices used in city infrastructure, the assistance of Smart City software is in the center of importance.

To develop a successful software system, a suitable and appropriate methodology should be chosen (Qureshi 2012). The term methodology corresponds to the systematic approach to a process, following a predefined plan and appropriate management that guarantees that planning is being respected. Any software development methodology is associated with the set of steps required to be executed with the aim of delivering the software or piece of software as a result. These steps are: requirements, design, coding, testing, roll-out, and maintenance (Qureshi 2012). During this software development lifecycle multiple models are being constructed (Elaasar and Conallen 2013). Specifically, different modelling techniques are employed in the requirements gathering stage of software development methodology and in the design step responsible for specifying how the information system will be implemented (Qureshi 2012). In general, modelling is an irreplaceable part of any system and serves a set of purposes: it helps to simplify reality, facilitate communication among stakeholders, and have different views on the system (Elaasar and Conallen 2013). To perform modelling there is a need for modelling languages that will determine: how the models must be created, their elements, notation, syntax, and semantics (Al-Fedaghi and Alahmad 2018). Smart City software is not an exception: It also requires a suitable software development methodology and modelling languages that support it.

Many papers have already discussed characteristics, advantages, and challenges of different software development methodologies (Vijayasarathy and Butler 2016) and modelling languages (Evensen and Weiss 2010). However, the investigation of existing studies has shown that there is a lack of literature dedicated to the description and comparison of different software development methodologies and modelling languages for a specific Smart City context. Therefore, the goal of this paper is to dig deeper into these two vital components of smart city software. More specifically, this paper is focused on answering the following three Research Questions (RQ):

- RQ1: What software development methodologies and modelling languages have been used or suggested to be used in Smart City projects?
- RQ2: What advantages do these methodologies and modelling languages bring?

– RQ3: What software development methodologies and modelling languages are now used in Belgian Smart Cities and what is the reason behind these choices?

## 2  Methodology

### 2.1  Literature Review

Since our first objective is to discover the current state of software development methodologies and modelling languages in Smart City context, literature review was considered a proper method to give an answer. To find articles that describe software development in Smart Cities we started with several combinations of the obvious search terms: *software development Smart City*. Based on this term the following queries were executed: *(software OR development OR projects OR process OR application OR method OR methodology) AND "Smart City"*. To extract specific information about modelling languages, we executed the following search query: *(design OR modelling) AND Smart City*.

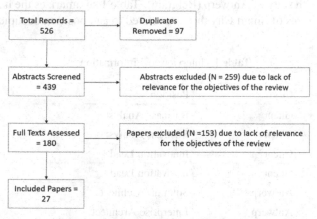

**Fig. 1.** Literature review methodology

The following inclusion criteria were developed: the study is written in English; the study is published between 2000–2020, to ensure that the article is recent and up to date; the study is cited in other research papers; the study cites other research papers; the study is written in a consistent and academic way; the study is aligned with the purpose of the literature review: it describes software development methodologies and/or modelling languages used in Smart Cities and reasons behind this choice. The most heavily used database was Google Scholar since it gives an extensive overview of the existing publications in multiple databases. Complementary searches were performed on other databases such as IEEE Xplore, Scopus and Web of Science. The procedure to select a study to be added to the paper is the following: first check the title and read the abstract. If the abstract of the paper is related to the purpose of the literature review, proceed with a full read of the paper; otherwise, discard it. If after full critical reading all inclusion criteria are met, the study is selected and utilized in the paper; otherwise, it is discarded. In total, as highlighted in Fig. 1, 27 papers were finally selected. 14 articles were selected for software development methodologies and 13 were selected for modelling languages. These papers can be found in the Appendix of this paper.

## 2.2 Interviews

To understand the use in practice in Belgium, we performed semi-structured interviews. This type of interview comprises a set of open-ended questions that tackle the topic the research aims at investigating. This research is considered beneficial since the open-ended nature of the questions identifies the focus of the interview yet provides room for a more detailed discussion between interviewer and respondent. The fact that the interview is not strictly structured permits to discover personal opinions and experience of the respondent (Guest et al. 2006). Six people participated in the interviews. Four of them were representatives of Smart City of Ghent (Belgium) and are employees of the organization named District09. District09 was defined by the respondents as the ICT provider for Ghent city. Other two respondents are employees of Digipolis Antwerpen, the IT partner of the city of Antwerp (Belgium). Table 1 summarizes the background of respondents in terms of Smart City they are related to and position occupied.

**Table 1.** Interviewees' information

| City | Position |
| --- | --- |
| Ghent | Business Analyst |
| Ghent | Business Analyst |
| Ghent | Innovation Lead |
| Ghent | Innovation Lead |
| Antwerp | Solution Architect |
| Antwerp | Enterprise Architect |

The type of qualitative data analysis that we have selected for this research is the-matic one. Thematic analysis was performed according to (Braun and Clarke 2014) and comprised six sequential steps: data familiarization, initial code generations, searching for themes, reviewing themes, defining and naming themes and producing the report. We started from transcribing recorded interviews into textual format. After this, interview transcripts were carefully read and meaningful units, recurrent ideas and main issues in data were highlighted. After thorough review of data, we performed initial coding by selecting relevant parts of text and assigning them a code name that captures the sense included in it. Coding executed has an inductive nature meaning that codes emerge pro-gressively from the data content and no codebook was developed in advance (Medelyan 2020). After the first round of coding was finished, the procedure was repeated to refine the code names and arrive with polished codes. Based on the acquired set of codes, we aimed at searching for themes by sorting initial codes into potential themes and sub-themes. The outcome of this step was a set of candidate themes, sub-themes and code associated with them. Next, themes and sub-themes were reviewed and refined making sure that they indeed capture what they were supposed to. Themes and sub-themes were then defined and renamed if necessary, highlighting the actual meaning stored in them and their differentiating characteristics. The coding scheme containing overarching themes, sub-themes, distinguishing characteristics, and example from transcript can be found in the supplementary material online[1].

## 3  Results

### 3.1  Methodologies and Modelling Languages in Smart City Projects

Based on our literature review related to software development methodologies, it was possible to identify three types of methodologies that were used or suggested to be used in different Smart City software projects: Traditional (Waterfall), Agile (General Agile, Scrum and AUP) and Hybrid Agile Methodology. Waterfall Model is characterized by sequential development, defined and clear requirements, testing only taking place after coding, documentation creation after each phase and test team involvement during the testing stage only. Agile is a framework that manifests client's satisfaction through continuous frequent delivery of functional software, welcomes changing requirements and encourages constant collaboration among motivated individuals. Table 2 illustrates the software methodologies that are being applied for different Smart City projects, the types of projects they were executed in, and the benefits (reported in the selected papers) of using them.

**Table 2.**  Software development methodologies

| Methodology | Applications | Benefits |
|---|---|---|
| Waterfall | Prototype of the smart office system for IOT-based security system | • easy to understand;<br>• easy to coordinate;<br>• structured documentation;<br>• minimal resources;<br>• easy implementation;<br>• quality of development process;<br>• minimized overhead;<br>• better cost estimation; |

*(continued)*

---

[1] https://zenodo.org/record/5887609#.Yeq08f7MI2w.

**Table 2.** (*continued*)

| Methodology | Applications | Benefits |
|---|---|---|
| Agile | • InterSCity Environmental monitoring system microservices-based platform (Custom Agile)<br>• Smart City Bus Application (Scrum)<br>• Blockchain- based software (Scrum)<br>• e-Rakorev Smart City Application (AUP) | • time and cost savings;<br>• less documentation;<br>• feedback from end-users;<br>• faster implementation;<br>• transparency;<br>• lightweight development process;<br>• rapid delivery of value;<br>• self-organizing team;<br>• acceptance of changing requirements;<br>• earlier data visualization |
| Hybrid-Agile Methodology (HAM) | Smart City Procurement | • allows to estimate time and budget;<br>• improved planning;<br>• resource sharing;<br>• reduced cost of misunderstanding and poor communication involvement of users;<br>• increases acceptation;<br>• educates citizens in project-related topic;<br>• strengthens citizens' interest in the city |

After investigation of modelling languages, we identified four modelling languages that were applied in different Smart City software development projects: UML, SysML, BPMN, DSML. Table 3 illustrates the software modelling languages that are being applied for different Smart City projects, the types of projects they were executed in and their reported benefits.

**Table 3.** Modelling languages

| Language | Application | Benefits |
|---|---|---|
| UML | • e-Rakorev Smart City Application<br>• Intelligent cloud-based car parking service<br>• Location aware mobile services for a Smart City | • common clarity about system operation;<br>• effective communication among stakeholders;<br>• guarantee that the correct system is being developed;<br>• support of the validation;<br>• traceability from requirements to low-level design |

(*continued*)

**Table 3.** (*continued*)

| Language | Application | Benefits |
|---|---|---|
| SysML | • Integrated Smart City System | • unambiguous;<br>• enforces consistency;<br>• prevents attempts at making incompatible connections;<br>• improves precision and efficient communication |
| BPMN | • Bike Sharing System<br>• Report broadcasted by police to citizens via the Telegram channel | • standardization;<br>• ease of use;<br>• rich set of symbols;<br>• no specific software required;<br>• improves business processes |
| DSML | • Smart Service System<br>• Citizen Mobility System | • increased modelling productivity;<br>• allows better coverage of the target domain;<br>• understood more easily by modelers and model users;<br>• use of expertise to share knowledge within the development team |

### 3.2   Methodologies and Modelling Languages in Belgium: State-of-Practice

**Software Development Methodologies**

All the respondents, both from Ghent and Antwerp, confirmed that their organizations try to be as Agile as possible and use Agile methodology most of the time. However, later participants explained that the development process is not completely Agile, even though it is called this. The requirements stage is completed in the Traditional Waterfall way, meaning that all the requirements are very detailed, clear, and consistent. The reason for this, as explained by our participants, is that Smart City projects are complex projects with many stakeholders involved and they are dependent on grants, funding, subsidies and on multiple governmental organizations that provide their support. When a proposal about the solution is created, it should include detailed, clear requirements and estimations to be present to relevant parties for approval. Business analysts from Ghent Smart City specified that when the new project initiation is received, they are responsible for conducting the whole research about the project and for producing a report containing all the strictly specified requirements, and a clear estimation of the timeline and budget needed. Antwerp representatives have also admitted that in the proposal that is being generated for their projects all requirements are very detailed, clear and are gathered and specified in Traditional Waterfall manner. The development itself, on the other hand, is being performed in Agile way with continuous incremental delivery. When asking about the reason for choosing this hybrid methodology, all respondents explained that the Traditional part of methodology applied to requirements is, first, required due to multiple stakeholders' dependency. Some Smart City representatives stated that, even though this way of dealing with requirements is necessary in Smart City projects, this method is also beneficial since it allows to avoid extra cost and time spending on modification of the solution.

**Modelling Languages**

All respondents mentioned that there is no standard modelling approach undertaken for software projects in their organizations and the selection of the models to be created depends on the business analyst responsible for their production and the characteristics of the project itself. Business analysts, as described by our respondents, are quite free to choose the way to deal with visualization of the requirement and design of the system. There are business analysts who create many different visualizations, while some business analysts barely create any models at all. When asking if the respondent find this unstructured modelling approach sufficient, we got an answer that it develops models that are clear, intuitive and understandable and this is far more important than sticking to strictly defined modelling languages. Therefore, practitioners focus more on understandability within their organization through ad-hoc modelling languages than one understandability in a broader context. Business analysts also underlined that there is no demand for standard UML diagrams since they require constant update. On the other hand, another business analyst from Ghent told us that he personally does not create any specific models. Business analyst, nevertheless, admitted that he can develop a Context Model sometimes. It was described as a useful model since it provides a useful overview of external factors and the system's interaction with them. Business analyst also explained that there is no specific modelling language applied for Context Models creation and named the approach used for this an "informal way" of models' generation. In favor of this modelling technique respondent stated that this approach is understandable, simple and allows for creativity. When investigating the challenges that are associated with certain modelling techniques, it was noticed that some of the respondents associate UML with complexity, maintenance that arises from changing requirements and time consumption. One of the participants said that: "We avoid UML models that require updates, maintenance, probably explanation even, we try to be high-level. Of course, different business analysts do this the way they consider it to be relevant. But no standards for this and no desire to spend time, effort, and money on structural modelling". One respondent also explained that BPMN-based models can sometimes be too complex or lack certain features. Therefore, the Service Blueprint is added as an extra model in this case. In general, participants tend to highlight that they are trying to avoid complex modelling, keep models clear, intuitive, lightweight and understandable. According to one of the respondents, "this is more important than the fact that I have to use strict analyst models". During one of the interviews, respondents suggested that focus should be shifted from the design stage, where these models are created, to the actual development and emphasis should be there. One more challenge that was announced and is not related to the specific modelling language, is the fact that advice about tooling is not given within the organization.

# 4 Discussion

Overall results of literature review led us to the conclusion that there is no specific methodology that fits all the Smart City software development projects. This finding is in line with the conclusions previously made in the literature related to the general software development projects (Vijayasarathy and Butler 2016). However, Hybrid Agile Methodology seems to be the most popular one in the Smart City projects performed by the interviewees. This makes sense as this method combines the benefits of the two other methods while addressing some of their challenges or limitations. With respect to the modelling languages, literature review results introduce four modelling languages implemented in multiple Smart City software projects: UML, SysML, BPMN and DSML. The findings with respect to the benefits demonstrate that all of the modelling techniques facilitate communication among stakeholders. UML leads to evasion of costly remarks and gives common clarity of the system, while SysML is unambiguous, scalable, consistent and allows to detect errors in early stages. BPMN is concluded to be easily understandable and facilitates involvement of the stakeholders. DSML, finally, is beneficial mainly due to its ability of customization for certain purposes, reliability, and reusability. One more important finding is that UML tends to be considered as time-consuming, expensive, effort demanding and can sometimes provoke miscommunication. When looking for modelling languages applied in Smart City projects in Belgium, some interviewees mentioned that did not always use models. This, consequently, leads us to assume that the modelling part could have been skipped in these projects due to the drawbacks mentioned above. As we can see from the results, all the modelling languages introduced by Smart City representatives serve the facilitation of communication among various parties which again supports the arguments illustrated in former studies (Elaasar and Conallen 2013).

Even though this paper provides a broad overview of software development methodologies and modelling languages in a Smart City context, this paper also has several limitations. The literature that refers to methodologies or modelling techniques in a Smart City context almost never explains the reasoning behind. Therefore, the answer to the second research question is more general and the link between the methodology or modelling technique chosen and the reasons behind this is missed. We tried to overcome this limitation by explicitly searching for the specific outcomes of the identified methodologies and modelling languages. The general lack of existing literature about the topic in the Smart City context shows that more research needs to be performed in this area. In addition, this study considers a limited number of interviewees (six people) of two Belgian Smart Cities, Ghent and Antwerp. This may have not allowed us to see a broader picture of possibilities and experiences. As such, in future work we suggest increasing the sample size to make results more representative. Moreover, we suggest making purposive sampling more accurate and direct the interviews towards more specific profiles. For example, when there is an aim to discover modelling techniques, it is suggested to consider business analysts, designers or modelers as a rich source of information.

## 5 Conclusion

This paper aimed at discovering software development methodologies and modelling languages applied in various Smart City projects, the reasoning behind their selection and have a closer look at the Belgian Smart Cities' experience with respect to these terms. From the literature study we discovered that Traditional (Waterfall), Agile (General Agile, Scrum, AUP) and Hybrid Agile are the methodologies applied for different Smart City projects. With respect to the modelling languages, we found UML, BPMN, SysML and DSML executed. Through the interview with Belgian Smart City representatives, we explored that they apply Traditional and Mixed methodology and execute UML, BPMN, ArchiMate, DSML and Informal modelling techniques. We also demonstrated benefits of the methodologies and modelling techniques derived from the literature and illustrated the experience of Belgian Smart Cities with respect to their approaches. While the limited number of respondents limits the generalizability of the findings, the paper provides valuable insight about possible approaches applied in Smart City context and sheds light on how Belgian Smart Cities manage software projects with respect to methodologies and modelling. Most importantly, it highlights justifications of the choices made and challenges faced by these Smart Cities. Further research is needed to discover software development methodologies and modelling languages implication in other Smart Cities and investigate how Smart City context influences the choice.

## Appendix: Selected Papers in the Literature Review

### Theme 1: Software Development Methodologies

Alshamrani, A., & Bahattab, A. (2015). A comparison between three SDLC models Waterfall Model, Spiral Model, and Incremental/Iterative model. *International Journal of Computer Science Issues (IJCSI)*, *12*(1), 106–111.

Balaji, S., & Murugaiyan, M. S. (2012). Waterfall vs. V-Model vs. Agile: A comparative study on SDLC. *International Journal of Information Technology and Business Management, 2*(1), 26–30.

Del Esposte, A. M., Kon, F., Costa, F. M., & Lago, N. (2017). InterSCity: A Scalable microservice-based open-source platform for Smart Cities. In M. Helfert, C. Klein, & B. Donnellan. (Eds.), *Proceedings of the 6th International Conference on Smart Cities and Green ICT Systems* (pp. 35–46).

Fong, S. L., Wui Yung Chin, D., Abbas, R. A., Jamal, A., & Ahmed, F. Y. (2019). Smart city bus application with QR code: a review. In *2019 IEEE International Conference on Automatic Control and Intelligent Systems (I2CACIS)* (pp. 34–39).

Ghilic-Micu, B., Stoica, M., & Mircea, M. (2014). Collaborative environment and agile development. *Informatica Economica, 18*(2/2014), 32–41.

Ibba, S., Pinna, A., Seu, M., & Pani, F. E. (2017). CitySense: Blockchain-oriented smart cities. In R. Tonelli (Ed.), *Proceedings of the XP2017 Scientific Workshops*.

Kaleshovska, N., Postolov, K., Janevski, Z., Josimovski, S., & Pulevska-Ivanovska, L. (2015). Contribution of scrum in managing successful software development projects. *Economic Development/Ekonomiski Razvoj, 17*(1–2), 175–194.

Karouw, S., & Wowor, H. (2013). e-Rakorev: Towards governance planning, monitoring and evaluation of urban development for Manado SmartCity. In 2013 International Conference on Advanced Computer Science and Information Systems (ICACSIS) (pp. 47–53)

Kishino, Y., Yanagisawa, Y., Shirai, Y., Mizutani, S., Suyama, T., & Naya, F. (2017). Agile environmental Monitoring Exploits rapid prototyping and in Situ Adaptation. *IEEE Pervasive Computing, 16*(2), 61–71.

Lom, M., Pribyl, O., & Zelinka, T. (2016). Hybrid-Agile Approach in Smart Cities Procurement. *20th World Multi-Conference on Systemics, Cybernetics and Informatics: WMSCI 2016.*

Prasetyo, T. F., Zaliluddin, D., & Iqbal, M. (2018). Prototype of smart office system using based security system. *Journal of Physics: Conference Series, 1013.*

Shankarmani, R., Pawar, R., S. Mantha, S., & Babu, V. (2012). Agile methodology adoption: Benefits and constraints. *International Journal of Computer Applications, 58*(15), 31–37.

Sharma, S., Sarkar, D., & Gupta, D. (2012). Agile processes and methodologies: A conceptual study. *International journal on computer science and Engineering, 4*(5), 892–898.

Vácha, T., Přibyl, O., Lom, M., & Bacúrová, M. (2016). Involving citizens in smart city projects: Systems engineering meets participation. In *2016 Smart Cities Symposium Prague (SCSP)* (pp. 1–6)

**Theme 2: Software Modelling Languages**

Ardito, C., Caivano, D., Colizzi, L., & Verardi, L. (2020). BPMN extensions and semantic annotation in public administration service design. In R. Bernhaupt, C. Ardito, & S. Sauer (Eds.), *Human-Centered Software Engineering* (pp.118–129).

Calderoni, L., Maio, D., & Palmieri, P. (2012). Location-aware mobile services for a Smart City: Design, implementation and deployment. *Journal of Theoretical and Applied Electronic Commerce Research, 7*(3), 74–87

Chaudron, M. R., Heijstek, W., & Nugroho, A. (2012). How effective is UML modeling? *Software & Systems Modeling, 11*(4), 571–580.

Cognini, R., Corradini, F., Polini, A., & Re, B. (2014). Modelling process intensive scenarios for the smart city. In M. Janssen, H. J. Scholl, M. A. Wimmer, & F. Bannister (Eds.), *Electronic Government* (pp. 147–158).

Dzidek, W., Arisholm, E., & Briand, L. (2008). A realistic empirical evaluation of the costs and benefits of uml in software maintenance. *IEEE Transactions on Software Engineering, 34*(3), 407–432.

Flowers, R., & Edeki, C. (2013). Business process modeling notation. *International Journal of Computer Science and Mobile Computing, 2*(3), 35–40.

Huber, R. X., Püschel, L. C., & Röglinger, M. (2019). Capturing smart service systems: Development of a domain-specific modelling language. *Information Systems Journal, 29*(6), 1207–1255.

Indulska, M., Green, P., Recker, J., & Rosemann, M. (2009). Business process modeling: Perceived benefits. In A. H. F. Laender, S. Castano, U. Dayal, F. Casati, J. P. M. de Oliveira (Eds.), *Conceptual Modeling - ER 2009* (pp. 458–471).

Ji, Z., Ganchev, I., O'Droma, M., Zhao, L., & Zhang, X. (2014). A cloud-based car parking middleware for iot-based smart cities: Design and implementation. *Sensors, 14*(12), 22372–22393.

Karouw, S., & Wowor, H. (2013). e-Rakorev: Towards governance planning, monitoring and evaluation of urban development for Manado SmartCity. In *2013 International Conference on Advanced Computer Science and Information Systems (ICACSIS)* (pp. 47–53).

Muvuna, J., Boutaleb, T., Baker, K. J., & Mickovski, S. B. (2019). A methodology to model integrated smart city system from the information perspective. *Smart Cities, 2*(4), 496–511.

Prasanna A. T. *A Domain Specific Modeling Language for specifying educational games* (Master's thesis) Vrije Universiteit Brussel. Faculty of Science, Master of Science in Applied Science and Engineering: Computer Science, Brussels.

Rosique, F., Losilla, F., & Pastor, J. Á. (2017). A domain specific language for smart cities. *Proceedings, 2*(3), 1–7.

# References

Ahvenniemi, H., Huovila, A., Pinto-Seppä, I., Airaksinen, M.: What are the differences between sustainable and smart cities? Cities (2017). https://doi.org/10.1016/j.cities.2016.09.009

Al-Fedaghi, S., Alahmad, H.: Integrated modeling methodologies and languages. In: ACM International Conference Proceeding Series (2018). https://doi.org/10.1145/3164541.3164605

Albino, V., Berardi, U., Dangelico, R.M.: Smart cities: definitions, dimensions, performance, and initiatives. J. Urban Technol. **22**(1), 3–21 (2015)

Braun, V., Clarke, V.: What can "thematic analysis" offer health and wellbeing researchers? Int. J. Qual. Stud. Health Well Being (2014). https://doi.org/10.3402/qhw.v9.26152

Caragliu, A., Del Bo, C., Nijkamp, P.: Smart cities in Europe. J. Urban Technol. **18**(2), 65–82 (2011)

Elaasar, M., Conallen, J.: Design management: a collaborative design solution. In: Van Gorp, P., Ritter, T., Rose, L.M. (eds.) ECMFA 2013. LNCS, vol. 7949, pp. 165–178. Springer, Heidelberg (2013). https://doi.org/10.1007/978-3-642-39013-5_12

Evensen, K.D., Weiss, K.A.: A comparison and evaluation of real-time software systems modeling languages. In: AIAA Infotech at Aerospace (2010). https://doi.org/10.2514/6.2010-3504

Gaur, A., Scotney, B., Parr, G., McClean, S.: Smart city architecture and its applications based on IoT. Procedia Comput. Sci. **52**(1), 1089–1094 (2015)

Guest, G., Bunce, A., Johnson, L.: How many interviews are enough?: An experiment with data saturation and variability. Field Methods **18**(1), 59–82 (2006)

Hollands, R.G.: Will the real smart city please stand up? City **12**(3), 303–320 (2008)

Medelyan, A.: Coding Qualitative Data: How To Code Qualitative Research. Thematic Analysis Inc. (2020)

Nam, T., Pardo, T.A.: The changing face of a city government: a case study of Philly311. Gov. Inf. Q. **31**(S1), S1–S9 (2014)

Qureshi, M.R.J.: Agile software development methodology for medium and large projects. IET Softw. **6**(4), 358–363 (2012)

Vijayasarathy, L.R., Butler, C.W.: Choice of software development methodologies: do organizational, project, and team characteristics matter? IEEE Softw. (2016). https://doi.org/10.1109/MS.2015.26

Zanella, A., Bui, N., Castellani, A., Vangelista, L., Zorzi, M.: Internet of things for smart cities. IEEE Internet Things J. **1**(1), 22–32 (2014)

# Domain Ontology Construction with Activity Logs and Sensors Data – Case Study of Smart Home Activities

Ramona Elali[1]([⊠]), Elena Kornyshova[2], Rébecca Deneckère[1], and Camille Salinesi[1]

[1] Paris 1 Panthéon Sorbonne, Paris, France
`ramona.elali@etu.univ-paris1.fr`, {`ramona.elali,`
`rebecca.deneckere,camille.salinesi`}`@univ-paris1.fr`
[2] Conservatoire National des Arts et Métiers, Paris, France
`elena.kornyshova@cnam.fr`

**Abstract.** Process mining relies on activity logs to discover process models, check their conformance, enhance processes, and recommend the next activity. On another side, many environmental factors such as time, location, weather, and profile are obtained from many sources, such as sensors, external systems, outside actors, or domain knowledge bases, and could also enhance recommendations. The existing research mainly focuses on single activity log datasets; only a few consider combining various sources. Our main goal is to provide better inputs to process discovery and better recommendations. In this paper, we focus on the combination of activity logs and sensors data with domain ontology as an intermediate step to attaining our goal. We use a case study of smart home activities to test this combination.

**Keywords:** Process mining · Ontology · Sensors · Events logs · Smart home

## 1 Introduction

An enormous amount of events data and sensor data is being recorded daily whilst the propagation of Information and Communication Technologies (ICT) is taking its rise worldwide across all domains. Data has become available everywhere, hence, the challenge becomes to turn out this data into value to get insight, increase productivity, produce better performance, and save costs [1].

Process Mining (PM) focuses on the generated activities from business processes that can be used as a recommendation technique to direct the user on which next activity to follow according to his current activity [2, 3]. PM's main objective is to discover, check the conformance, and enhance the process models that are based on event logs [1].

Ontology is an important subject in the domain of IS [4]. Many researchers are using ontology to classify domain knowledge [5] such as concepts, all types of entities, and the existing relationships between them [6]. Ontology organizes information in a natural, logical, and systematic way. Therefore, contextual information can be structured into

J. Horkoff et al. (Eds.): CAiSE 2022, LNBIP 451, pp. 49–60, 2022.
https://doi.org/10.1007/978-3-031-07478-3_4

a domain ontology by describing the relationships between the entities of the domain ontology and the contextual information.

In this paper, we propose an approach that combines events logs with contextual data obtained from sensors by using domain ontologies. Nowadays, contextual data can be obtained through many techniques and from various sources. We believe that contextual data can enrich the event logs by providing insights about users' behavior. We test and illustrate this proposal by applying it to a case study of Smart Home daily living activities. We choose this specific case study because this domain is rich in contextual information due to the presence of many sensors. Hence, we use the dataset provided by BP-Meets-IoT 2021 Challenge [7]. This dataset contains an event log of the activities of daily living in addition to the sensor's log data. We are focusing on this case study to construct a specific domain ontology that identifies the links between the different person's activities and the sensor's data.

The next section will focus on the related works. Section 3 will present our proposal which we illustrate in Sect. 4. We conclude in Sect. 5.

## 2  Related Works

PM purposes to enhance, improve, discover, or check the conformance of activity-oriented process models from event logs [1, 2]. Event logs are the main input of information for the mining techniques [25].

However, PM approaches do not usually take into account the context aspect behind the recorded user activities. By using various sources of logs, the discovered process models can offer better guidance through processes. In [26], a process mining approach is suggested in the context of sensor data where sensor data were transformed into event logs to be used as input in the PM techniques. A comprehensive review on event logs preparation techniques from raw of data was introduced in [27]. In this review, the authors describe three steps of data preparation: event data extraction from heterogeneous data sources, event correlation, and event abstraction.

Ontology is now widely used in the Information Systems and Artificial intelligence world [6], where many researchers classify concepts, entities, and the relationship between different concepts in domain knowledge [5, 6]. An ontology-based personalized recommender approach to provide a more precise and personalized recommendation was presented in [8]. In [9], a combination between the ontology-based recommender system and machine learning techniques is used to provide a personalized recommendation for students. An ontology-based recommendation approach relying on collaborative filtering that achieves a better recommendation in e-Learning systems was presented in [10]. In [11], a classification for research papers was done using ontology then they used collaborative techniques to recommend to the users interesting papers. In addition, activity recognition in Smart Home is a crucial topic to study while working on process mining. In [4], the authors proposed a hierarchical ontology to annotate the human activity in a home environment for healthcare taking into consideration the social context of the activity, the room, and the physical state. [12] developed a knowledge-driven approach by creating ontologies for the sensors and the activities for the purpose of activity recognition. In addition, in [13], they have developed an ontology for the activities of daily living in a smart environment to use as input for a supervised learning technique for online activity recognition. Also, an Activity of a Daily Living ontology-based approach was developed in [14, 15] for activity recognition in a context-aware smart home environment.

## 3    Approach to Combine Sensors Data and Event Logs Using Domain Ontology

In our view, we believe that ontologies can help to combine sensors data and activity logs. Firstly, all the data acquired from the sensors and all the activities of the events log can be semantically interpreted in an ontology specific to the domain. Secondly, all the links between the ontology concepts (especially the links between the sensors elements and the activities elements) must be defined. For instance, a specific value of sensor data can trigger the start, or the end, of an activity.

To combine sensors data and event logs using domain ontology we have to proceed in three steps (see Fig. 1): (1) create the sensor ontology based on the sensors data, (2) create the activity ontology based on the events log and (3) refine the domain ontology by creating the links between the two preceding ontologies (white arrow on the second part of Fig. 1).

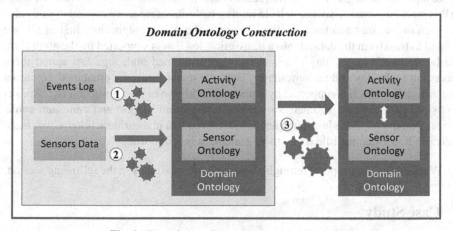

**Fig. 1.**  Domain ontology construction approach.

If the events log and the sensor data are related to existing ontologies, we can proceed directly to step 3 to identify the links between them.

In this work, we focus on step 3 with two main hypotheses: **H1:** *It is possible to identify the ontological links between sensors data and activities using the timestamp on data and events.* **H2:** *It is possible to identify the ontological links between sensors data and activities by association rules.*

**Timestamps.** The timestamp is considered the only attribute that can let us find the relationship between the activity event and the sensor. We developed a Python algorithm that takes as input the events log and sensor log. The two logs need to be sorted according to the timestamp field. This algorithm is composed of two main steps. In the first step, the start and completion of each activity should be identified. Then, the timestamp field is used to pivot the events log according to the start and completion of each activity. Then in the second step, a join was done between the two logs using the timestamp field to create the link between the sensor data and the event data.

**Association Rules.** Association rule mining is the technique of finding relationships between different items. It is commonly used in Market Basket Analysis, where it identifies which items are frequently purchased together for marketing purposes. It is the process of finding frequent patterns, associations, causal structures, and correlations within different datasets existing in different types of databases like transactional databases, relational databases, or any other form of databases [16, 17]. The purpose of association rule mining is to find the rules that allow us to guess the appearance of a specific item after the occurrences of other items in the transaction. It is one of the top concepts of machine learning rule-based techniques that discover interesting relations between items in big databases by indicating the frequent associations' rules that are composed of an antecedent and consequent [16]. Association rules allow uncovering the hidden relationships between the items that are frequently used together. It is represented by if-then statements (an antecedent itemset and a consequent itemset). Apriori [18] is one of the top standard algorithms for frequent itemset mining and association rule learning. In this work, we used Association Rule mining techniques since we needed to find rules between the sensors and the activities. To apply the Apriori algorithm, first of all, we needed to transform the dataset into a transaction log that is supported by the algorithm. We labeled each log by day date and then we combined both logs and sorted them according to the day and the timestamp. Then we transformed the combined log into a transaction log which is supported by Apriori. In addition to the transaction log, Apriori needs as input multiple parameters such as the minimum support and minimum confidence. *Support* indicates how often an itemset is frequent in the transactions. *Confidence* indicates how often the rule (if → then) statement is found true.

We illustrate our proposal through a Smart Home case study in the following section.

## 4   Case Study

The rapid evolution of artificial intelligence endorses the existence of smart homes and make it crucial to study this domain. Numerous studies are done on smart home [19–22]. Hence, our case study will be focused on smart home since this field is rich in different types of sensors. We need to find the link between the person's activities and the sensors to find later how the context can affect the user's intention. Data preprocessing includes standard activities aiming at enhancing data quality: cleaning, integration, and transformation [23].

In our experiment, we are using the dataset provided by BP-Meets-IoT 2021 Challenge [7]. This dataset consists of two people's activities logs in addition to the sensor logs recorded during 21 consecutive days between 16 March 2020 and 6 April 2020. While studying the dataset, we found 53 activities and 16 sensors. Both logs contained noise data; some duplicated records, in addition to some records that don't represent any type of activities or sensors. We cleaned the dataset from the noise by removing those tuples, and we obtained 23166 records in the events log and 39304 records in the sensors log. A sample of each of the datasets is shown in Fig. 2. Each record in the event logs is identified by the Activity Name while each record in the sensor logs is identified by the Sensor Name and both logs are categorized by the Timestamp and the Resource Id.

Event Logs:

| ActivityName | ResourceId | Timestamp | Transition | EventId | CaseName | TraceId | Position | Day |
|---|---|---|---|---|---|---|---|---|
| go_wardrobe | 2 | 2020-03-16 00:00:00+00:00 | complete | 4071 | sleeping_BP | 435 | wardrobe | Day1 |
| get_clothes | 2 | 2020-03-16 00:00:00+00:00 | start | 4072 | sleeping_BP | 435 | wardrobe | Day1 |
| get_clothes | 2 | 2020-03-16 00:01:00+00:00 | complete | 4076 | sleeping_BP | 435 | wardrobe | Day1 |
| change_clothes | 2 | 2020-03-16 00:01:00+00:00 | start | 4077 | sleeping_BP | 435 | wardrobe | Day1 |
| change_clothes | 2 | 2020-03-16 00:05:00+00:00 | complete | 4080 | sleeping_BP | 435 | wardrobe | Day1 |
| go_bathtub | 2 | 2020-03-16 00:05:00+00:00 | complete | 4081 | sleeping_BP | 435 | bathroom_sink | Day1 |

Sensor Logs:

| SensorName | ResourceId | Timestamp | EventId | Day | Value | Position |
|---|---|---|---|---|---|---|
| position | 1 | 2020-03-16 00:01:00+00:00 | 18 | Day1 | 1202 852 | wardrobe |
| position | 1 | 2020-03-16 00:06:00+00:00 | 24 | Day1 | 1184.75270036629 848.333251258976 | |
| water_use | 0 | 2020-03-16 00:07:00+00:00 | 25 | Day1 | 10 | |
| position | 1 | 2020-03-16 00:07:00+00:00 | 27 | Day1 | 1246 638 | wc |
| water_use | 0 | 2020-03-16 00:31:00+00:00 | 51 | Day1 | 1 | |
| position | 1 | 2020-03-16 00:31:00+00:00 | 53 | Day1 | 1164 768 | bathroom_sink |

**Fig. 2.** Event logs and sensor logs samples.

There was not any defined domain ontology given with the dataset. Moreover, despite previous works already having defined ontologies for the daily activity recognition in smart homes [4, 12–15], none of them were matching the data of our dataset. Thus, we had to define this domain ontology ourselves. After a deep analysis of the data of the sensors and events log, we were able to identify the different parts of the domain ontology. To construct our domain ontology - which is specific to our dataset and case study - we have defined two main ontologies (Smart home activity ontology – Subsect. 4.1 and smart home sensor ontology – Subsect. 4.2). Their links are detailed in Subsect. 4.3. To ease the understanding of our work, we propose here only a simplified view of the two ontologies where all the links between the concepts are "is-a" relationships. We define the more complex associations between the concepts in a specific meta-model (cf. Fig. 10).

## 4.1 Smart Home Activity Ontology

The Activity ontology (Fig. 3) contains the different types of activities and actions that can happen inside a home.

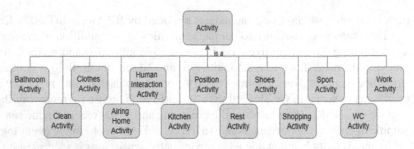

**Fig. 3.** Smart home activity ontology.

Each activity should be completed by a human inside a fixed location. The Activity ontology is divided into groups of activities (see Fig. 3): Bathroom Activity, Clean Activity, Work Activity, etc... Each activity group inside the Activity ontology has its own instances. As an example, the Kitchen Activity has a set of real-life activities that happen inside the kitchen (see Fig. 4). Drink Water, Go Kitchen Shelf, Put Plate to Sink, Wash Dishes, etc... are instances of Kitchen Activity group.

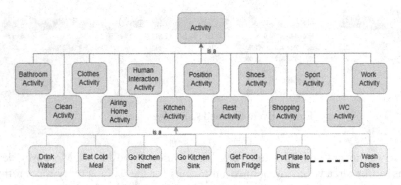

**Fig. 4.** Smart home activity ontology with details about the kitchen activity.

### 4.2 Smart Home Sensors Ontology

Smart Home Sensors Ontology includes three parts: Sensor, Position, and Human ontologies.

The sensor ontology contains all the information related to the sensors such as sensor type, value, value range, and location. According to our dataset, we were able to identify different types of sensors such as Environment sensors, Kitchen Sensors, etc. In Fig. 5, we have presented the high level of the ontology sensor, where the sensors are divided into different types and each type contains its related sensors.

For each location inside the home, there are a set of sensors related to the location such as Kitchen Sensor, Bedroom Sensor, and Living Room Sensor. And there are some sensors that are common to all the house as the Environment Sensor, Power Sensor, and Water Sensor.

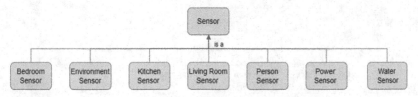

**Fig. 5.** Sensor ontology high level.

Figure 6 shows an example of instances of Kitchen Sensor. Fridge Door Contact Sensor, Cooked Food Sensor, Food Sensor, and Unwashed Dishes Sensor are all sensors located inside the kitchen. Each sensor works differently according to its type, and it has its own range of values [7]. For instance, the Unwashed Dishes sensor is used to count the number of unwashed dishes inside the kitchen sink, its value is greater than 0 when there are dishes inside the sink to wash, otherwise, it will be 0. While the Fridge Door Contact Sensor indicates when the fridge door is opened or closed, so its value is 0 when it is closed and 1 once it is opened. The Food Sensor is used as a food counter inside the home, so its value is equal to or greater than 0. As for the Cooked Food Sensor, it works the same as the Food Sensor, but it counts only the available cooked food inside the home.

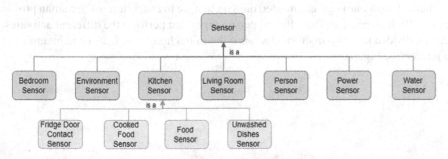

**Fig. 6.** Kitchen sensor instances example.

Position ontology (Fig. 7) represents the different parts of the home where the activities can take place and the sensors are attached. Position ontology is divided into 6 main positions categories (see Fig. 8): Entrance Position, Exercise Place Position, Bathroom Position, Kitchen Position, and Living Room Position.

Each position category has its own instances that represent the different fixed locations inside the home. As an illustration, the Kitchen Position contains the different positions inside the conditions such as the dining table, the fridge, the kitchen shelf, and the kitchen sink (see Fig. 8).

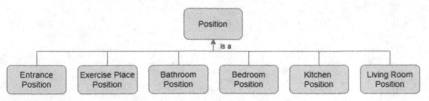

**Fig. 7.** Position ontology high level.

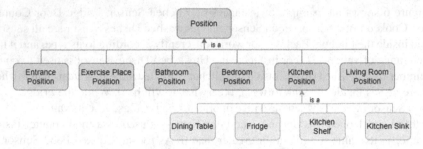

**Fig. 8.** Kitchen position instances example.

Then, Human ontology is a needed domain to have to characterize the human profile (see Fig. 9). It categorizes the different person types that perform the different activities. It can be divided into two main subdomains: the initial home residents (inhabitants) and the guests (see Fig. 9).

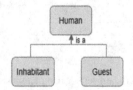

**Fig. 9.** Human ontology high level.

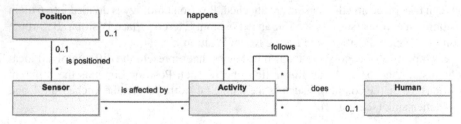

**Fig. 10.** Links between the ontologies.

### 4.3  Links Between Sensors and Activity Ontologies

We can identify different relationships between the defined ontologies (see Fig. 10). Each human does activities. Sensors affect activities and can be positioned at a specific position. Each activity can be followed by one or many activities (that can be done sequentially or not). Each activity can happen at a particular position at home and be affected by sensors. Each position can be related to sensors and activities.

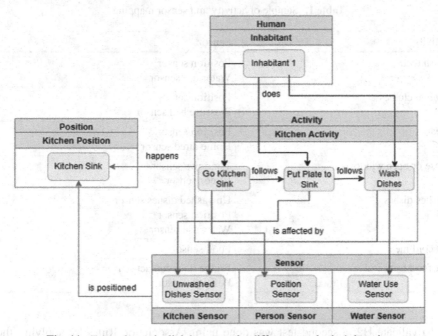

**Fig. 11.** Example on the link between the different ontologies' domains.

Figure 11 illustrates an example of the links between the ontologies. When the human' goal is Washing Dishes then the set of activities that are related to this goal will take place inside the kitchen; the inhabitant will go to the kitchen sink, put the plate inside the sink and start to wash dishes. In the meantime, the sensor of Unwashed Dishes will increase its value according to the plates that are being washed. The Water Use sensor will increase its value and the Position sensor will indicate that the human position is next to the Kitchen Sink.

The established relationships were used to test the established hypotheses. As presented in Sect. 3, we had two main hypotheses: it is possible to identify the ontological links between sensors data and activities using the timestamp on data and events (H1), and it is possible to identify the links by association rules (H2).

To validate H1, an automatic test was done using Python as a programming language. 100836 records were obtained corresponding to 53 different activities and 16 different sensors. The obtained data was cleaned because it was containing some noise data thus the remaining was 99975 records. We obtained 112 correspondences between activities and sensors. We compared the mapping results with the results that we obtained manually while analyzing the data and deduced that for each occurred activity there is one or multiple sensors triggered. An extraction is given in Table 1 to illustrate the obtained links between activities and sensors using the timestamp data (the complete list can be found in [24]). In this manner, we were able to validate H1 and identify the link between the activities and the sensors while relying only on the timestamp.

**Table 1.** Sample of activity and sensor mapping.

| Activity | Sensor |
| --- | --- |
| Brush teeth | Position sensor<br>Water use sensor |
| Change clothes | Position sensor<br>Pressure bed sensor |
| Clean | Position sensor<br>Home aired sensor |
| Close or open windows | Windows sensor<br>Blinds sensor |
| Washes dishes | Unwashed dishes sensor<br>Position sensor<br>Water use sensor |
| Eat cold meal | Food sensor |
| Get food from fridge | Fridge door contact sensor<br>Position sensor |

To validate H2, a second test was done using Association Rules by applying the Apriori algorithm [18] on the dataset selecting only the logs that are relevant to one person. After combining the logs, we obtained 410 transaction records. We did three experiments. We set the confidence value to 80% in all the experiments to get strong rules. The minimum support value is set through the process of trial and error. In the first experiment, we set the value of minimum support to 0.15 and we obtained 56 rules. In the second experiment, we set the minimum support value to 0.05 and we obtained 8565 rules. And in the third experiment, we set a small value of minimum support equal to 0.03 and we obtained 34623 rules. We analyzed the generated rules manually and found that the result of the second experiment is more realistic due to the value of the minimum support and the confidence. In Table 2, we present a small extraction of the obtained rules [24] with the corresponding confidence degrees for each rule.

Thus, despite the limitation of Apriori to perform well when the itemset is large, we were able to generate rules that associate activities with sensors and validate H2.

On the whole, this experiment has validated the existing relationship between the sensors and the activities. We were able to automatically find the rules that we have found before manually while analyzing the dataset. For an instance, when a person goes to the kitchen next to the shelf; the position sensor will locate his position accordingly, so the next activity will be to get a glass then move to the sink where the 'water use' sensor will directly reflect the water consumption while filling the glass with water. And after drinking water, the 'unwashed dishes' sensor will increment its value.

**Table 2.** Sample of the obtained rules.

| Rule | Confidence |
|---|---|
| {eat_cold_meal_go_kitchen_shelf, go_fridge, fridge_door_contact_sensor} → {position_fridge_sensor, food_sensor, get_food_from_fridge} | 0.92 |
| {position_kitchen_sink _sensor, water_use _sensor} → {drink_water} | 0.92 |
| {go_computer_chair, go_computer, position_computer_chair_sensor} → {switch_computer_on, power_use_sensor} | 0.83 |

## 5  Conclusion

This research paper describes an approach to constructing domain ontologies using sensors data and events logs. Sensor, Position, Human, and Activity are the ontologies that were defined. Our main objective in this work was to find relations between sensors and activities. We were able to identify and validate the link between sensor data and activities, based on a Smart Home case study. However, the limited amount of data prevented us to find more interesting links between activities and sensors.

A future experiment on a larger dataset will provide us with a more complete set of links Then, we will continue our main research proposal by using these ontologies as input to build process models by precising the links between sensors and activities in order to identify which data can trigger an activity. Our main goal is to be able to make recommendations to users on the fly, following these contextual data and the event logs.

## References

1. Aalst, W.M.P.: Process Mining: Data Science in Action. Springer, Heidelberg (2016). ISBN: 978-3-662-49850-7
2. Khodabandelou, G., Hug, C., Deneckère, R., Salinesi, C.: Process Mining Versus Intention Mining. In: Lecture Notes in Business Information Processing, vol. 147, pp. 466–480. Springer, Heidelberg (2013)
3. Compagno, D., Epure, E., Deneckere, R., Salinesi, C.: Exploring digital conversation corpora with process mining. Corpus Pragmatics **2**, 1–23 (2018)
4. Woznowski, P., King, R., Harwin, W., Craddock, I.: A human activity recognition framework for healthcare applications: ontology, labelling strategies, and best practice, pp. 369–377 (2016)
5. Mansingh, G., Osei-Bryson, K.M., Reichgelt, H.: Using ontologies to facilitate post-processing of association rules by domain experts. Inf. Sci. **181**(3), 419–434 (2011)
6. Viinikkala, M.: Ontology in information systems. In: Computer Science (2004)

7. Koschmider, A., Leotta, F., Serral, E., Torres, V.: BP-Meets-IoT 2021 Challenge Dataset (2021)
8. Ge, J., Chen, Z., Peng, J., Li, T.: An ontology-based method for personalized recommendation. In: 2012 IEEE 11th International Conference on Cognitive Informatics and Cognitive Computing, Kyoto, Japan, pp. 522–526 (2012)
9. Obeid, C., Lahoud, I., Khoury, H., Champin, P.A.: Ontology-based recommender system in higher education. In: 2018 Web Conference Companion (WWW 2018), France (2018)
10. Zhang, Z., Gong, L., Xie, J.: Ontology-based collaborative filtering recommendation algorithm. In: Liu, D., Alippi, C., Zhao, D., Hussain, A. (eds.) BICS 2013. LNCS (LNAI), vol. 7888, pp. 172–181. Springer, Heidelberg (2013). https://doi.org/10.1007/978-3-642-38786-9_20
11. Middleton, S.E., Roure, D.D., Shadbolt, N.R.: Ontology-based recommender systems. In: Staab, S., Studer, R. (eds.) Handbook on Ontologies. IHIS, pp. 779–796. Springer, Heidelberg (2009). https://doi.org/10.1007/978-3-540-92673-3_35
12. Chen, L., Nugent, C., Wang, H.: A knowledge-driven approach to activity recognition in smart homes. IEEE Trans. Knowl. Data Eng. 24, 1 (2012). https://doi.org/10.1109/TKDE.2011.51
13. Salguero, A., Espinilla, M., Delatorre, P., Medina, J.: Using ontologies for the online recognition of activities of daily living. Sensors 18 (2018)
14. Chen, L., Nugent, C.: Ontology-based activity recognition in intelligent pervasive environments. IJWIS 5, 410–430 (2009)
15. Bae, I.: An ontology-based approach to ADL recognition in smart homes. Futur. Gener. Comput. Syst. 33, 32–41 (2014)
16. Zaki, M.J., Meira Jr., W.: Data Mining and Analysis: Fundamental Concepts and Algorithms (2014)
17. Aher, S.M.D.A., Lobo, L.M.R.J.: A comparative study of association rule algorithms for course recommender system in E-learning. Int. J. Comput. Appl. 39, 48–52 (2012). https://doi.org/10.5120/4788-7021
18. Agrawal, R., Srikant, R.: Fast algorithms for mining association rules. In: Proceedings International Conference Very Large Data Bases (VLDB), pp. 487–499, September 1994
19. Tiwari, P., Garg, V., Agrawal, R.: Changing world: smart homes review and future. In: Moh, M., Sharma, K.P., Agrawal, R., Garcia Diaz, V. (eds.) Smart IoT for Research and Industry. EICC, pp. 145–160. Springer, Cham (2022). https://doi.org/10.1007/978-3-030-71485-7_9
20. Alam, M.R., Reaz, M.B.I., Ali, M.A.M.: A review of smart homes - past, present, and future. IEEE Trans. Syst. Man Cybern. Part C Appl. Rev. 42, 1190–1203 (2012)
21. De Silva, L.C., Morikawa, C., Petra, I.M.: State of the art of smart homes. Eng. Appl. Artif. Intell. 25, 1313–1321 (2012)
22. Alaa, M., Zaidan, A.A., Zaidan, B.B., Talal, M., Kiah, M.L.M.: A review of smart home applications based on Internet of Things. J. Netw. Comput. Appl. 97, 48–65 (2017)
23. Tamilselvi, R., Sivasakthi, B., Kavitha, R.: An efficient preprocessing and postprocessing techniques in data mining. Int. J. Res. Comput. Appl. Rob. 3(4), 80–85 (2015)
24. Elali, R.: Data exploration of BP-Meets-IoT 2021 challenge dataset: correspondences & associations rules result. White Paper, University of Paris 1 Panthéon-Sorbonne (2022)
25. Diaz-Rodriguez, O.E., Perez, M., Lascano, J.: Literature review about intention mining in information systems. J. Comput. Inf. Syst. 61, 1–10 (2019)
26. Van Eck, M.L., Sidorova, N., Van der Aalst, W.M.: Enabling process mining on sensor data from smart products. In: 2016 IEEE Tenth International Conference on Research Challenges in Information Science (RCIS), pp. 1–12. IEEE, June 2016
27. Diba, K., Batoulis, K., Weidlich, M., Weske, M.: Extraction, correlation, and abstraction of event data for process mining. Wiley Interdisc. Rev. Data Min. Knowl. Discovery 10(3), e1346 (2020)

# Empirical Analysis of Technology Acceptance of Private Electric Vehicle Charging Infrastructure in Germany

Tim Deumlich[1], Martin Amberger[1], and Omid Tafreschi[2(✉)]

[1] Frequentum GmbH, Hammersbacher Street 7, 81377 Munich, Germany
{tim.deumlich,martin.amberger}@frequentum.com
[2] Darmstadt University of Applied Sciences, Haardtring 100, 64295 Darmstadt, Germany
omid.tafreschi@h-da.de

**Abstract.** Private charging infrastructure is critical to the diffusion of electric vehicles. However, as with all technologies, user acceptance is of primary importance here. This paper analyzes this acceptance with an empirical study with 488 participants. For this, a context-specific technology acceptance model including 9 hypotheses is developed. To validate the hypotheses, an online survey is designed for the German market. Results deliver insights on the general opinion on electromobility and private charging infrastructure and determine the factors influencing the acceptance behavior of potential users with regard to private charging infrastructure. Regarding the general opinion, most of the survey participants show a positive attitude. Regarding the factors, some, such as perceived effort and perceived usefulness, have an influence on the acceptance, while other factors, such as visual design and perceived cost, don't.

**Keywords:** Electric vehicles · Private charging infrastructure · User acceptance

## 1 Introduction

As early as 2013, Markkula et al. identified high prices, short operational range, and lack of charging infrastructure as key challenges for electromobility [1]. From today's perspective, their forecasts with regard to falling prices and increasing ranges are valid [2]. The problem of lack of charging infrastructure still exists and is one of the main barriers for the adaption of electric vehicles (EV) [3]. Charging EV differs significantly in terms of time from refueling conventional vehicles. Therefore, it is necessary to consider the user acceptance when charging an EV [4]. Here, the divergent requirements of mobility must be considered. This results in different needs for charging EV, which are to be covered by a range of technical solutions as described by [5]. For example, in terms of accessibility, [5] distinguishes between private, e.g., private parking space at home, semi-public, e.g., at the supermarket, and public, e.g., on public roads. A private electric vehicle charging infrastructure (PEVCI) can be used exclusively, e.g., by a household [6]. This has a visible interface, i.e., home charging station, and typically provides a

J. Horkoff et al. (Eds.): CAiSE 2022, LNBIP 451, pp. 61–72, 2022.
https://doi.org/10.1007/978-3-031-07478-3_5

maximum charging power of 22 kW. In terms of charging requirements, the movement profile of vehicles must be considered. According to [7], vehicles are parked at home most of the time. These long parking durations can reduce the demands on the required charging power and enable smart charging. In addition, private charging can lead to a gain in convenience [8] and spur the digital transformation of mobility. However, according to [9] a new technology such as a PEVCI can only be accepted if potential users have positive experiences with it. Specifically, with regard to electromobility, this is confirmed by [10, 11]. For these reasons, we address the following research questions in this paper:

1. What is the general opinion on electromobility and private charging infrastructure?
2. What factors influence the acceptance behavior of potential users with regard to private charging infrastructure?

To answer these questions, Sect. 2 develops a new context-specific model for acceptance behavior using existing models for analyzing user acceptance and formulates corresponding hypotheses. In addition, a quantitative empirical analysis is conducted in Sect. 3 to test the formulated hypotheses. As part of the empirical analysis, a survey is designed, conducted, and analyzed. The results are then presented in Sect. 4, after which related work is discussed in Sect. 5. Finally, a conclusion is drawn, and an outlook is given in Sect. 6.

## 2 Technology Acceptance Model

The Technology Acceptance Model (TAM) has its origins in Davis' dissertation in 1985 [12]. According to the model modified by Davis et al. depicted by Fig. 1, actual system use depends on the external variables of a system and the intention to use, which is determined by the perceived usefulness, the perceived ease of use, and the attitude toward system use of the respective user.

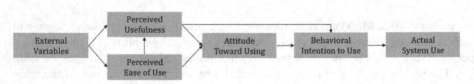

**Fig. 1.** TAM 1 [13]

A study conducted by Davis revealed previously unknown correlations between the variables [14]. According to [15], perceived ease of use and perceived usefulness have a direct influence on behavioral intention to use. Furthermore, the assumed link between attitude toward using and behavioral intention to use could be rejected as not significant. For these reasons, the component of attitude toward using is not considered in later modifications of the TAM [15].

The structure of TAM has been confirmed by [16, 17]. The original model was enhanced several times by Davis and other authors. Starting with TAM 1 [13], TAM 2 [18], the unified theory of acceptance and use of technology (UTAUT) [19], and TAM 3 [20] were developed over the following 19 years. In general, it can be noted that a large number of subsequent research papers have directly used TAM 1 or modified it for their purposes, despite its extensive extensions [17, 21, 22]. Due to its simplicity and flexibility, contextual applicability, TAM 1 still serves as the basis for TAM-related research contributions [15, 17, 22]. For these reasons, we use TAM 1 to develop a specific technology acceptance model, i.e., context-specific TAM, for analyzing the use of PEVCI. For this, we propose necessary new constructs and use approved constructs of mentioned TAM developments.

The constructs perceived usefulness (PU) and behavioral intention to use (BI) are adopted unchanged from TAM 1. Perceived ease of use is renamed perceived effort (PE) because more of the added constructs can be combined under this term. PE is the cost, organizational, or time effort that a person associates with using the charging system. The following hypotheses emerge from the three constructs mentioned above:

H1: The stronger the PU, the more likely the BI the charging system.
H2: The lower the PE, the more likely the BI the charging system.
H3: The lower the PE, the greater the PU of the charging system.

Actual system use is also used according to TAM 1, but this is not examined as part of the empirical analysis. The construct external variables is modeled in more detail here or replaced by several, new constructs, which are explained below.

Output quality (OQ) was taken from TAM 2 and TAM 3. It indicates the degree to which a person trusts a system to perform a corresponding task to their satisfaction [23]. In the present context, this means to what extent a potential user trusts that his PEVCI will charge his electric car sufficiently, in a certain time, and according to his imagination. The following hypothesis is proposed:
H4: The better the OQ, the greater the PU of the charging system.

Perceived convenience (PCon) is a new construct in the proposed context-specific TAM. It is defined as the comfort that a person expects when using the charging system. Thus, the following hypothesis emerges:
H5: The higher the PCon, the greater the PU of the charging system.

The construct of visual design (VD) is also introduced as a new construct of our context-specific TAM. The VD represents the user's subjective perception of how appealing the appearance of the charging system and especially the home charging station is perceived to be, or whether the VD contributes a decisive factor to the PU. Within the context of this construct, the following hypothesis is stated:
H6: The more aesthetic and attractive the VD of the charging system, the greater its PU.

Another new construct is environmental awareness (EA), which is a characteristic of the user. According to [24], EA is defined as "insight into the endangerment of the natural basis of life by humans themselves, combined with the willingness to take remedial action." The decisive factor here is the willingness to take remedial action. The following hypothesis was developed:

H7: The more the potential user's EA, the greater the PU of the charging system.

The construct experience (E), i.e., the experience in relation to electromobility, is found in the approved further developments of the TAM and adapted in the context-specific TAM. In this model, E refers to the level of experience or knowledge of the potential user of electromobility in general and PEVCI in particular. The following hypothesis is put forward:

H8: The broader user's E in electromobility in general and the charging system in particular, the lower the PE.

The construct perceived costs (PCost) represents another construct developed as part of the context-specific TAM and depends on financial resources and usage needs. It does not examine the actual costs incurred, but the subjectively perceived costs:

H9: The lower the PCost of the charging system, the lower the PE.

We propose the construct external variables (ExV) analogous to the approaches of Davis et al. [13] and Venkatesh et al. [19]. In this paper, ExV is understood as sociodemographic structural data. These can have an influence on PU and PCost. However, since many different aspects have an influence on the ExV, no explicit hypothesis is made at this point.

Figure 2 shows the context-specific TAM. The relationships between the constructs other than ExV are indicated by hypotheses H1-H9.

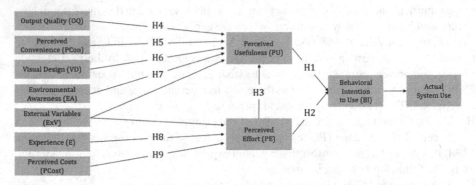

**Fig. 2.** Context-specific TAM

## 3   Research Design

The data for the empirical analysis were collected in an online survey during January 2021. The survey consisted mainly of closed questions to ensure a clear evaluation of the data obtained [25]. In the introductory questions, the general opinion of the participants on electromobility was queried, which serves to answer the first research question. For this, participants were asked first for positive and then for negative associations with electromobility. The participants were also asked about their living situation and whether they already owned an EV. Depending on the answer, the further course of the survey was adjusted, e.g., in contrast to the others, owners of EV were asked how they charge their vehicles.

Likewise, specific questions were asked about the constructs developed from the context-specific TAM. The goal was to explore the factors that influence acceptance behavior or intention to use, which answers the second research question.

Next, the participants were asked about the ExV. It consisted of socio-demographic structural data, i.e., year of birth, gender, highest level of education, monthly net income, living arrangements, i.e., rental/ownership, number of inhabitants.

In the context of structural equation models, so-called hypothetical constructs have to be tested and measured. As a rule, these are complex and mostly mental matters that cannot be measured easily. For this purpose, the constructs have to be operationalized. Directly observable indicators (items) are identified in order to develop the constructs. The constructs can then be made measurable by a linear combination of the items, which serve as auxiliary variables [22, 26].

In order to measure the items, a suitable scale must be used. The most common scales for measuring attitudes in social science surveys are verbalized or endpoint-named scales with four to seven scale points. For endpoint-named scales, the outer points of the scale are named, e.g., I disagree, I agree. The other scale points are treated as if they were equally spaced. Thus, a scale that is actually ordinally scaled becomes an interval scale, which facilitates the evaluation of the items [25]. According to [25], the best-known psychometric scales of this type are so-called Likert scales [27]. Thus, the Likert scale was chosen. This scale was to be six-point as recommended by [26] since it is not possible to swerve to the middle with an even number of response options.

The endpoints were described as "do not agree" and "fully agree". With the help of this scale, the participants were able to evaluate the given items or statements. The first three scale points were taken as a negation of the statement, the last three as an agreement. The answer options and the scale points for all items were numbered from 1 to 6 for reasons of clarity, comparability and evaluation.

To ensure the comprehensibility and content relevance of the items [13, 28], construct operationalizations validated in the literature were used. These items were adapted to the context of "charging electric vehicles". Only for the self-developed constructs, new items had to be created. Table 1 shows some selected constructs and their assigned items including their sources.

The choice of the sample size is crucial for the success of an empirical analysis [26]. The sample is a selection of cases, e.g., a subset of a population [26]. We use the formula for calculating the sample size proposed by [33], resulting in 384 participants, which are sufficient according to the meta-analysis conducted by [34] and the recommendation of [35].

**Table 1.** Operationalization of the constructs

| Construct | Items | Sources |
|---|---|---|
| PU | "I find it useful to be able to charge an electric vehicle at home." (v_50) <br> "Private charging infrastructure at home is a good idea." (v_51) <br> "Being able to charge at home is more convenient than refueling an internal combustion vehicle at a gas station." (v_52) | [19, 29] <br> New item |
| PE | "I imagine charging an electric vehicle to be easy." (v_103) <br> "I don't see much difficulty in operating a home charging station." (v_104) | [19, 29] |
| OQ | "I assume that charging my electric vehicle with a home charging station will work at home." (v_106) <br> "I assume that charging my electric vehicle with the help of a home charging station will be sufficient." (v_107) <br> "I assume that electrical short circuits and cable fires will be avoided." (v_108) | [18, 30–32] |
| PCon | "Driving to gas stations on a regular basis is annoying for me." (v_115) <br> "I save time when I can charge at home." (v_116) | New item <br> New item |

## 4 Results

669 participants took part in the survey, 559 of whom completed it (completion rate = 83.56%). After unsuitable data records, e.g., those with contradictory statements, were sorted out during data cleaning, the data set finally included N = 488 usable interviews. On this basis, further analysis were conducted. More men (68%) than women participated in the survey. The average age of survey participants was 36 years. The youngest participant was 18 and the oldest was 78 years old. Most participants have either no parking space or a public parking space available (37.3%). 28.1% park in the garage, 6.6% in underground parking, and 27.9% have an outside parking space.

For reliability tests, Cronbach's alpha coefficients [36] for all constructs are calculated. The reliabilities of the constructs PE and PCost are questionable. Therefore, individual items of these two constructs are omitted, which improves the coefficient. All results of reliability tests are now ranked between acceptable and excellent. Only the internal consistency of the construct PE can still be classified as questionable.

For the explorative factor analysis, the intercorrelation between all 29 items of the constructs is tested. The result of the factor analysis is a rotated component matrix. The matrix shows how strongly each item loads on the different factors. The loadings can be interpreted as correlations. In the present case, 7 factors exist, which explain a total variance of 69%.

Ideally, the items of a construct would load on the same factor, which is the case for constructs E, EA, VD, and PCost. However, the results of the intercorrelation tests show two anomalies concerning three constructs. First, the items of the constructs PE and OQ load on the same factor. For this reason, the constructs OQ and PE were merged. The items of OQ are another aspect of PE, because if a technology does not bring the expected OQ, the user would have additional effort to achieve a better OQ. Consequently, he has more effort. Because PE is more relevant to the study than OQ and, furthermore, is involved in 3 hypotheses, the OQ items are added to the construct PE. OQ is a component of hypothesis H4, so it must be rejected in advance. Second, the item v_52 of the construct PU loads onto the factor as all items of the construct PCon. Therefore, this item is assigned to the construct PCon. In order to test the reliability of the newly composed constructs, the Cronbach's alphas are determined, which results in an even better reliability. The new compositions do not have any further effects for the other hypotheses. Based on the factor analysis, the items of a construct can now be combined by calculating the arithmetic mean to simplify further analysis.

Regarding the first research question "What is the general opinion on electromobility and private charging infrastructure?", the participants name many positive, but also many negative aspects. Over 60% of participants rate the low exhaust emissions, a quiet engine, and the technology's future orientation as positive (see Fig. 3).

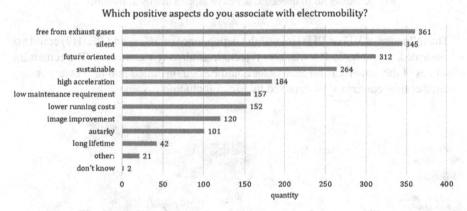

Which positive aspects do you associate with electromobility?

| | |
|---|---|
| free from exhaust gases | 361 |
| silent | 345 |
| future oriented | 312 |
| sustainable | 264 |
| high acceleration | 184 |
| low maintenance requirement | 157 |
| lower running costs | 152 |
| image improvement | 120 |
| autarky | 101 |
| long lifetime | 42 |
| other: | 21 |
| don't know | 2 |

**Fig. 3.** Absolute frequencies: positive aspects of electromobility

Participants rate low ranges, the insufficient number of charging options and the high purchase costs for EV as negative aspects (see Fig. 4). There are also concerns about the sustainability of EV. Above all, battery production, the resources required for this and disposal are viewed critically.

The participants' knowledge of EV is average (arithmetic mean = 3.5) and their knowledge of home charging stations is rather poor (arithmetic mean = 2.7). The low level of experience may mean that the positive and negative associations are not fact-based, but are the result of assumptions or claims made by third parties. Most participants (94%) assume that the PEVCI works, adequately meets their charging needs, and is safe. The corresponding construct OQ was rated an average of 5.3. This represents one aspect of the acceptance of home charging stations.

To answer the second research question "What factors influence the acceptance behavior of potential users with regard to private charging infrastructure?", the hypotheses H1–H9 developed in Sect. 2 were analyzed. The hypotheses were tested using a linear regression analysis.

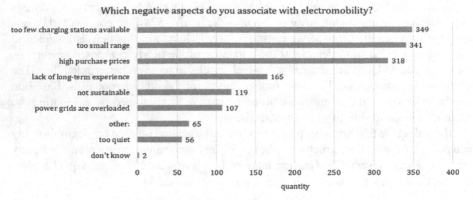

**Fig. 4.** Absolute frequencies: negative aspects of electromobility

The influence of VD on PU (H6) and the dependence of PCost and PE (H9) could not be confirmed. Hypothesis H4 was also rejected, as already mentioned. The remaining influences of the constructs on each other could be demonstrated and the corresponding hypotheses thus confirmed as depicted by Fig. 5 including p-values.

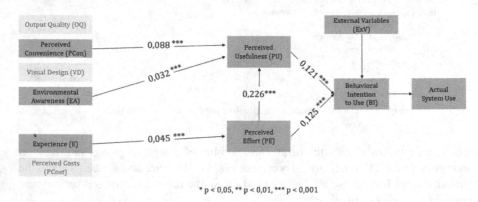

**Fig. 5.** Context-specific technology acceptance model

ExV such as the residential and parking space situation can influence the intention to use. In order to demonstrate this influence, other approaches were used in addition to the regression analysis. In particular, the results of an additional conducted cluster analysis, consideration of the reasons for non-use of home charging stations, and groupings of the sample based on socio-demographic structural data showed the dependence of intention to use on ExV. The influences can be seen as follows: parking spaces are considered a prerequisite for the use of PEVCI. In contrast to single-family houses, the implementation of PEVCI in multi-family houses is because of the necessary load management, power distribution, and consumption-based billing complicated and more expensive. As a result, 46% of the participants, who do not want to use home charging stations, see their living situation in multi-family housing or the missing parking space as an obstacle. Although influences of ExV on the intention to use were shown, no linear relations could be demonstrated. Dependencies between the other constructs (PE, PU) and the ExV could not be proven. A direct influence between income and intention to use could not be proven, but the EV users are relatively wealthier compared to all participants. They have on average about 40% more income.

## 5 Related Work

As early as 2011, [4] recognized the relevance of user acceptance for electromobility and explained why it is crucial for the diffusion of electromobility in addition to solving technical prerequisites. According to the empirical study [4], users will charge vehicles primarily at home or at work. However, the acceptance factors for PEVCI are not investigated. The attractiveness of private charging is also confirmed by [8], which uses 20 interviews to investigate how users evaluate the different options for charging and how charging can be integrated into daily routines, as this integration is a prerequisite for acceptance. The interview results confirm that home charging is the most attractive option for users. However, in contrast to our work, this option is not analyzed in more detail. Analogous to our approach, [22] also uses TAM to investigate the factors for the acceptance of electromobility. Here, car sharing in particular is considered in a differentiated manner. The general influence of charging infrastructure on acceptance is also investigated and confirmed, but private charging is not considered. [6] considers business models for charging service operators. For this, three alternative scenarios with different charging services as well as charging station ownership and accessibility are developed and analyzed. The results confirm the financial attractiveness of PEVCI, but the factors influencing its adoption are not analyzed. The research results confirm that private home charging is likely to be the preferred option for EV users as it offers lower total cost of ownership under certain conditions. However, the design of PEVCI is not addressed. [10] also investigates user acceptance for successful adoption of electromobility. The authors examine the attitudes of users and differentiate between users with purchase intentions and actual users who have experience with EV. Among other things, the topic of charging in general is addressed. The research results show that real experiences have a positive influence on the acceptance of EV. The analysis of the acceptance of electromobility is also the subject of [37]. For this purpose, the authors conduct an empirical study comparing traditional vehicles and EV. The results show that traditional vehicles are still perceived as much more convenient. The limited availability of charging stations is identified as a major reason against EV. According to [11], it is essential to understand users' requirements for charging locations and their individual charging behavior. For this reason, the authors investigate users' requirements for fast charging stations. The results demonstrate that waiting time for an available charging station, charging costs, and the necessary detour to reach a charging station are the key attributes from the users' perspective. These results confirm the need for our research, as private charging can meet the aforementioned requirements.

## 6  Conclusion and Outlook

The aim of the paper was to obtain an opinion on electromobility as well as PEVCI and to identify factors influencing the acceptance behavior of potential users regarding PEVCI. For this purpose, Davis' TAM was chosen as the basis for developing a context-specific TAM for PEVCI. Based on this model 9 hypotheses were formulated, which have been validated with an empirical analysis including 488 usable datasets. By analyzing the answers to the questions about positive and negative associations with electromobility, the picture of opinion toward electromobility became clear. Overall, electromobility is seen as a future-oriented, sustainable technology, but many participants are not yet satisfied with the ranges of EV, the number of charging options and the high purchase costs for EV. However, the criticized aspects are currently undergoing a positive change. Some participants clearly doubt the actual sustainability of EV and justify this primarily with the energy-intensive battery production, the resource procurement required for this and the disposal. The survey revealed a high level of expectation towards home charging stations. The participants assume that home charging stations work, can meet the charging needs of a private user and are safe. This is an important prerequisite for the acceptance of home charging stations.

Based on the analysis conducted, some expected factors influencing the acceptance behavior of PEVCI were confirmed, while others were rejected. It was found that the VD of a home charging station has no influence on the PU. Furthermore, no relationship between PCost and PE could be identified. The positive influence of PCon as well as EA on PU was confirmed with a small coefficient of determination. In addition, PE was shown to decrease with increasing E. The relationships between PE, PU and BI, which are known from other TAM studies, could also be confirmed in the context of PEVCI. Last, influences of ExV such as the parking space situation or housing conditions on the BI were identified. However, there were no linear correlations. It should be emphasized that, overall, many different framework conditions and factors have an influence on the acceptance behavior towards PEVCI.

Our results enable further research by more specific surveys considering the increasing awareness of electromobility. This kind of survey could analyze the wishes and concerns of certain user groups, such as multi-family home residents, regarding the technical as well as the economic implementation of charging solutions to develop sustainable business models with, for example, intelligent charging control.

## References

1. Markkula, J., Rautiainen, A., Jarventausta, P.: The business case of electric vehicle quick charging - no more chicken or egg problem. In: World Electric Vehicle Symposium and Exposition (EVS 27), vol. 2013, pp. 1–7 (2013)
2. Horváth & Partners: Status quo der E-Mobilität in Deutschland (2020). https://www.hor vath-partners.com/de/media-center/studien/faktencheck-e-mobilitaet-status-quo-der-e-mob ilitaet-in-deutschland-update-2020/
3. International Energy Agency: Global EV Outlook 2021. Accelerating ambitions despite the pandemic (2021)

4. Peters, A., Hoffmann, J.: Nutzerakzeptanz von Elektromobilität. Eine empirische Studie zu attraktiven Nutzungsvarianten, Fahrzeugkonzepten und Geschäftsmodellen aus Sicht potenzieller Nutzer (2011)
5. Kley, F., Lerch, C., Dallinger, D.: New business models for electric cars—a holistic approach. Energy Policy **39**, 3392–3403 (2011)
6. Madina, C., Zamora, I., Zabala, E.: Methodology for assessing electric vehicle charging infrastructure business models. Energy Policy **89**, 284–293 (2016)
7. Nobis, C., Kuhnimhof, T.: Mobilität in Deutschland (2018). http://www.mobilitaet-in-deutsc hland.de/pdf/MiD2017_Ergebnisbericht.pdf
8. Daubitz, S., Kawgan-Kagan, I.: Integrated charging infrastructure: cognitive interviews to identify preferences in charging options. Eur. Transp. Res. Rev. **7**(4), 1–14 (2015). https:// doi.org/10.1007/s12544-015-0184-2
9. Endruweit, G. (ed.): Wörterbuch der Soziologie. UTB Soziologie, vol. 8566. UVK-Verl.-Ges, Konstanz (2014)
10. Schneider, U., Dütschke, E., Peters, A.: How does the actual usage of electric vehicles influence consumer acceptance? In: Hülsmann, M., Fornahl, D. (eds.) Evolutionary Paths Towards the Mobility Patterns of the Future. Lecture Notes in Mobility, Springer, Berlin, pp. 49–66 (2014). https://doi.org/10.1007/978-3-642-37558-3_4
11. Philipsen, R., Schmidt, T., Ziefle, M.: Well worth a detour? - Users' preferences regarding the attributes of fast-charging infrastructure for electromobility. In: Stanton, N.A., Landry, S., Di Bucchianico, G., Vallicelli, A. (eds.) Advances in Human Aspects of Transportation. Advances in Intelligent Systems and Computing, vol. 484, Springer, Cham, pp. 937–950 (2017). https://doi.org/10.1007/978-3-319-41682-3_77
12. Davis, F.D.: A technology acceptance model for empirically testing new end-user information systems: Theory and results (1985)
13. Davis, F.D., Bagozzi, R.P., Warshaw, P.R.: User acceptance of computer technology: a comparison of two theoretical models. Manage. Sci. **35**, 982–1003 (1989)
14. Davis, F.D.: User acceptance of information technology: system characteristics, user perceptions and behavioral impacts. Int. J. Man Mach. Stud. **38**, 475–487 (1993)
15. Arnold, C., Klee, C.: Akzeptanz von Produktinnovationen. Springer Fachmedien Wiesbaden, Wiesbaden (2016). https://doi.org/10.1007/978-3-658-11537-1
16. Schepers, J., Wetzels, M.: A meta-analysis of the technology acceptance model: investigating subjective norm and moderation effects. Inf. Manage. **44**, 90–103 (2007)
17. Olbrecht, T.: Akzeptanz von E-Learning: eine Auseinandersetzung mit dem Technologieakzeptanzmodell zur Analyse individueller und sozialer Einflussfaktoren (2010)
18. Venkatesh, V., Davis, F.: A Theoretical extension of the technology acceptance model: four longitudinal field studies. Manage. Sci. **46**, 186–204 (2000)
19. Venkatesh, V., Morris, M.G., Davis, G.B., Davis, F.D.: User acceptance of information technology: toward a unified view. MIS Q. **27**, 425–478 (2003)
20. Venkatesh, V., Bala, H.: Technology acceptance model 3 and a research agenda on interventions. Decis. Sci. **39**, 273–315 (2008)
21. Shen, D., Laffey, J., Lin, Y., Huang, X.: Social influence for perceived usefulness and ease-of-use of course delivery systems. J. Interact. Online Learn. **5**, 270–282 (2006)
22. Fazel, L.: Akzeptanz von Elektromobilität. Springer Fachmedien Wiesbaden, Wiesbaden (2014). https://doi.org/10.1007/978-3-658-05090-0
23. Davis, F.D., Bagozzi, R.P., Warshaw, P.R.: Extrinsic and intrinsic motivation to use computers in the workplace 1. J. Appl. Soc. Psychol. **22**, 1111–1132 (1992)
24. Feess, E., Günther, E.: Definition: Umweltbewusstsein. Springer Fachmedien Wiesbaden GmbH, Wiesbaden (2018)
25. Porst, R.: Fragebogen. Ein Arbeitsbuch. Springers, Wiesbaden (2014). https://doi.org/10. 1007/978-3-658-02118-4

26. Döring, N., Bortz, J.: Forschungsmethoden und Evaluation in den Sozial- und Humanwissenschaften. Springer, Berlin (2016). https://doi.org/10.1007/978-3-642-41089-5
27. Likert, R.: A technique for the measurement of attitudes. Arch. Psychol. **140**, 5–55 (1932)
28. Hornburg, C., Giering, A.: Konzeptualisierung und Operationalisierung komplexer Konstrukte. Ein Leitfaden für die Marketingforschung. Marketing ZFP **18**, 5–24 (1996)
29. Davis, F.D.: Perceived usefulness, perceived ease of use, and user acceptance of information technology. MIS Q. **13**, 319 (1989)
30. Chang, S.-C., Tung, F.-C.: An empirical investigation of students' behavioural intentions to use the online learning course websites. Br. J. Edu. Technol. **39**, 71–83 (2007)
31. Roca, J.C., Chiu, C.-M., Martínez, F.J.: Understanding e-learning continuance intention: an extension of the technology acceptance model. Int. J. Hum Comput. Stud. **64**, 683–696 (2006)
32. Shin, D.: An empirical investigation of a modified technology acceptance model of IPTV. Behav. IT **28**, 361–372 (2009)
33. Cochran, W.G.: Sampling Techniques. Wiley, New York (1963)
34. Legris, P., Ingham, J., Collerette, P.: Why do people use information technology? A critical review of the technology acceptance model. Inf. Manage. **40**, 191–204 (2003)
35. Boomsma, A.: The robustness of LISREL against small sample sizes in factor analysis models Systems under indirect observation, pp. 149–173
36. Cronbach, L.J.: Coefficient alpha and the internal structure of tests. Psychometrika **16**, 297–334 (1951)
37. Ziefle, M., Beul-Leusmann, S., Kasugai, K., Schwalm, M.: Public perception and acceptance of electric vehicles: exploring users' perceived benefits and drawbacks. In: Marcus, A. (ed.) DUXU 2014. LNCS, vol. 8519, pp. 628–639. Springer, Cham (2014). https://doi.org/10.1007/978-3-319-07635-5_60

# A Sustainability Matrix for Smartphone Application

Amal Alsayed[1] and Rébecca Deneckère[2(✉)]

[1] RTE (Réseau de Transport d'Électricité), Paris la defense, France
[2] Centre de Recherche en Informatique, University Paris 1 Panthéon-Sorbonne, Paris, France
denecker@univ-paris1.fr

**Abstract.** Nowadays, smartphones are an indispensable part of most people's lives, they are a means of enabling communication and exchange that makes everyone comes together. However, it comes with a cost as the production and use of these systems is affecting the global earth ecosystem. Considerations about sustainability are more and more in people minds and the possibility to offer sustainable smartphone applications can be an asset to any company. We propose in this work a sustainability matrix for Smartphone applications in order to identify their sustainability degree and offer some new thinking to their project managers. We created this matrix with a state of the art study, expert interviews and a public questionnaire. We then tested our matrix on a real application.

**Keywords:** Sustainability · Smartphone · Application · Criteria · Matrix

## 1 Introduction

Technologies are progressing considerably to meet the ever-increasing needs of humans. However, we know that this quest for progress has harmful effects on environment and therefore on humanity. One of the most threatening impacts is ecological. A large majority of scientists agree on the severity of climate change [1]. Increase in the average temperature at the globe surface, decrease in soil fertility, ice melting at the poles are effects which must be limited as far as possible and as soon as possible. There is clear evidence that information technologies contribute to this environmental impact and climate change [2]. Living a smart life comes now with a smart way to handle the life cycle of technological products in the best possible way.

The strategy followed by companies to reduce these effects is called Green IT. However, even if it presents huge potential on the corporate level [3], there is little research regarding its application and potential outside organizations [4]. In this field, it has been shown that the production of products traditionally represents a factor of 100 in relation to their use. If the environmental issue is based on making a material sustainable, then we can wonder if the software and its life cycle cause the premature renewal of terminals. [5] states that *"Most of the figures available today show that digital power is responsible for 3.7% of the world's total greenhouse gas (GHG) emissions in 2018 and 4.2% of global primary energy consumption. Worldwide, 44% of this footprint is due to the*

J. Horkoff et al. (Eds.): CAiSE 2022, LNBIP 451, pp. 73–85, 2022.
https://doi.org/10.1007/978-3-031-07478-3_6

*manufacture of terminals, computer centers and networks and 56% to their use."* The equipment life cycle consists of several steps that begin with prefabrication and end with the end of life of the equipment [6]. Each step has its own impact on the environment. The prefabrication phase has the greatest impact on the environment, since it requires the extraction of non-renewable materials, followed by the use phase [6]. The latter has an impact on the environment because of the induced energy consumption. We believe that software can cause the premature renewal of terminals. This comes in many forms, like the disproportionate demand for machine resources (due to poor design and/or software development), the impact of software and the demands of associated hardware devices (misuse) or a contribution to programmed obsolescence.

Considering the average population of a developed country and its collective uncon-sciousness, people believe that software, due to its lack of physical existence, would have no direct impact on the environment. To demonstrate the opposite, it is enough to recall that the hardware stores information (hard drive, USB drive), and runs the software that operates calculations to render services (processors, memory, etc.). These elements have an impact on the environment at every stage of their life cycle. Therefore, to accept this hypothesis or reject it, we must measure the influence of software to determine its impact on equipment and therefore environmental impacts.

The turnover of technologies, hardware, etc. is such today that it may seem vain to want to make a software sustainable. On the one hand, the definition of sustainability focuses more on the environmental impact than on the objective of making software last for a long time. On the other hand, some works shows that it is possible to design a software incorrectly, to develop it incorrectly, to use it incorrectly and to leave a strong residual imprint [7, 8]. Our purpose is therefore to propose a mobile app sustainability matrix that outlines the criteria for software sustainability. Ideally, this matrix will allow us to determine whether a software is sustainable or not. There are several families of software but we restricted our work mainly on the SmartPhones software family.

Section 2 gives some information about the background. Our research methodology is explained in Sect. 3 with an identification of the sources of our defined criteria. Our proposed sustainability matrix is then completely defined in Sect. 4 and evaluated in Sect. 5. We conclude in Sect. 6.

## 2 Background

One of the most common interrogation nowadays is how to preserve the environment. How can we reduce greenhouse gas pollution and decrease the percentage of carbon dioxide in the air? The concept of Sustainability has been applied in several areas such as real estate [9], home appliances [10], marketing [11], transportation [12] and so on. Of course, one of those areas is information technology, which in turn tries to reduce its negative impact on the environment [13]. Sustainable Management is the long-term process of optimizing environmental, economic and social performance simultaneously while taking into account natural resource restrictions, This allows business to continue without compromising the needs of future generations [14].

We have to make a clear distinction between Information Technology and Infor-mation Systems (IS). *Information Technology* refers to all that is computer hardware, software or peripheral information equipment. *Green Information Technology* refers to measures and initiatives that aim to reduce the negative environmental impact resulting from the manufacture, operation and disposal of IT equipment and infrastructure [14]. *Information System*, on the other hand, is a broader concept that covers both technological components and human activities related to the process of managing and using technology within the organization. Information technology affects our environment in many different ways. Every stage of a computer's life, from its production to its disposal and use, poses environmental problems. Each computer used generates approximately one ton of carbon dioxide each year [15]. *Green Information Systems* refers to practices that aim to reduce the negative environmental impacts of IS, business operations and IS-based products and services. All this by determining how we use to invest, deploy, use and manage IS [14].

We have to better understand the IT environmental impacts and how to make our IT infrastructures, products, services, operations, applications and practices environmentally friendly. [15] proposes to apply Green IT on four several ways: Green use (to reduce the energy consumption of computers and other IS), Green disposal (to refurbish, reuse or recycle old computers), Green design (to design energy efficient and environmentally sound components, computers, servers, and cooling equipment), and Green manufacturing (to manufacture electronic components with minimal or no impact on the environment). Talking about software durability makes no sense if one does not consider the durability of the hardware on which they are instantiated. The ecological footprint depends on the equipment durability. There are many types of computer hardware, such as computers, smartphones, video game consoles, televisions connected to a box, connected objects, etc. Each type has an ecological footprint.

There are several studies that clarify the ecological footprint concept. One of these studies is the GreenIT.fr team's Global Digital Environmental Footprint [16], which focuses on quantifying the global digital environmental footprint and its evolution between 2010 and 2025. This study applies to all electronic equipment that manipulates binary data. The methodology followed is based on Life Cycle Analysis, and has quantified environmental impacts based on three categories (users, networks, computer centers) that are aggregated by a meta-model. The four indicators considered in this study are: [16] Abiotic Resource Depletion (impact of technology on the depletion of mineral stocks), Global Warming (climate change), Energy balance (the "primary" energy is the energy required to produce the final energy), and tension on Fresh Water (after breathing air, fresh water is classified as the second most important basic physiological resource also for humans than for other life forms).

As explains in [2], ICTs and all computer equipment account for between 2 and 10% of carbon dioxide emissions according to the studies, with an agreement around 4–105%. However, aviation accounts for about 2% of carbon dioxide emissions. Studies show that both manufacturing and recycling phases are responsible for the highest proportion of carbon dioxide emissions. Hence the importance of coupling between hardware and software to develop sustainable softwares.

Software sustainability alone is not enough to make hardware durable. At the same time, there are also prerequisites for the durability of the equipment. It appeared that the software, by its poor design, makes the computer hardware obsolete faster than expected

[7]. From a general perspective, the life cycle of computer hardware can be segmented into five major phases: [6] Prefabrication, Manufacture, Distribution and Transport, Use, End of life. All the phases are important when talking about sustainability [17].

Some works exists on environmental sustainable mobile applications, as stated in a literature review presented in [18]. Some applications provide feedbacks about sustainability information on an application but are restricted to specific domains, whereas others facilitates sustainable behaviors. [18] categorized the identified applications by their goals and functionalities to provide an overview of existing user-centric Green IS solutions from IS research and practice. They assessed the potentials of mobile applications to contribute to environmental sustainability and provide a holistic perspective by performing an extensive classification of existing apps.

Applications like Ecometer[1], GTmetric[2] or EcoIndex[3] for instance, proposes a free analyze of a website sustainability. Quentic[4] proposes a customizable sustainability software to track and manage environmental compliance online. All these services use some criteria that can be rapidly characterized in order to provide a quick feedback.

Some literature reviews [19, 20] concentrates on the decision making point of view to handle sustainability criteria and compare multicriteria methods used in the literature on this domain.

## 3   Research Methodology

Every phase of a computer life cycle, from manufacturing to construction or recycling, has an impact on the environment. This is why Green IT is responsible for studying each phase separately and finding more sustainable solutions. We will restrict our work on this research on the two first phases of software lifecycles, namely the design and the development. Once the research question was identified, to identify the more important criteria for smartphone software sustainability, we conducted a state of art literature review (SoA), interviews with experts and launched a questionnaire. We then used the found criteria to create a sustainability matrix that we tested on a real case.

**Identification of the Research Question.** Our hypothesis is that the lifecycle of a software can cause the renewal of the hardware. We stated that we have to measure the influence of the said software to determine its impact on equipment and therefore environmental impacts. Our research question is then the following: *Is it possible to evaluate a mobile application, based on predefined criteria, to identify its sustainability?*. We think that this question will particularly interest project managers to include good practices into future software developments. We specifically address in this work the software family of smartphones and the two first phases of a software lifecycle (design and development).

---

[1] http://www.ecometer.org/.
[2] https://gtmetrix.com/.
[3] http://www.ecoindex.fr/.
[4] https://www.quentic.com/sustainability-software/.

**Literature Study: State of Art.** Many works proposes criteria of sustainability for IS, softwares or websites. It allowed us to select several criteria (cf. Table 1).

A survey [21] revealed that programmers had limited knowledge of energy efficiency, were not aware of best practices for reducing software energy consumption and were not sure how software consumes energy. This issue becomes very important with the growing popularity of mobile computing and the emergence of large-scale cloud deployments.

The energy behavior of a smartphone has been studied in detail in [22]. According to the results, the biggest energy consumers are the GSM module and the display, including LCD panel, touch screen, accelerator/ graphics driver and backlight. The results indicate that audio consumes a large portion of static consumption, in the range of 28-34mW. Overall, RAM, audio, and SD card have little effect on the electrical consumption of the device and therefore offer little potential for energy optimization.

[7] proposes a practical guide to think about sustainable computing holistically, starting with the choices you make when buying technology, through to the software and peripherals you use, how you store and work with information, manage your security, save power, and maintain and dispose of your old hardware. It looks at the use of IT from the viewpoint of the information which the system manipulates.

[23] propose a label called EcoSoft that looks into stakeholders involvement (project manager, software architects, developers) in the integration of sustainability into a project. The three stages of the software's life cycle, namely the development, usage and end of life, were analyzed to determine the environmental impacts they generate. The analysis focus on the energy consumption of software components, which is an important aspect for the overall quality of the software, especially for the user experience on the mobile device, but also because digital energy consumption has a high environmental footprint.

[8] proposes a review about Energy Consumption & IT systems, starting from the view-point of Green IT. They introduce a taxonomy of concepts, present recent data on energy consumption trends and some guidelines to write energy efficient software.

**Qualitative Study: Interviews.** Seven experts working at RTE in the R&D and DSIT departments were selected to be interviewed (Green IT managers, IT department managers, IT developers). Questions asked were fairly open to cover as much as possible aspects related to the issue raised. The interviews were rich in information and focused on the main points to be raised when dealing with the subject of Green-IT. During these interviews several substantive criteria to optimize the performance of the software were determined (cf. Table 1).

One criteria that popped up in the interviews as a very high concern about sustainability is the programmed obsolescence (the fact that some applications are designed to be "out of date" when the devices are getting older), also widely discussed in [7]. However, this criteria is not so easy to identify and we decided not to include it in our matrix. Another criteria concerning the other phases of the lifecycle appears in the answers, like an excessive use of the battery or the performance on devices.

**Quantitative Study: Questionnaire.** A questionnaire was conducted to collect the criteria that make the software more sustainable or not according to the developers. There were two main sections. The first provides information on respondents' years of experience and programming languages. It also lets you know whether respondents are smartphone app developers or not. The second allows to know if the developers take into account the energy consumption, and to collect the criteria that allow to build the sustainability matrix. In addition, this section includes two open-ended questions for developers to suggest ways to assess the sustainability of software and technical design methods. 33 persons answered the questionnaire. The results showed that developers had different levels of experience with a higher representation of more than 10 years and 3 to 5 years of experience. In addition, the most commonly used programming languages are: Java, C++ and Python, with a lower representation of: Objective C, Swift and KotLin.

The difference in the level of experience of the developers indicate that the participants do not have the same knowledge of how the software consumes the resources of the machine and, consequently, the awareness of energy consumption. This is also confirmed by the results of the fourth question: Do you take into account energy consumption when developing software? If so, how do you account for energy consumption? Most of the answers showed a definite interest in this problem, but a difficult implementation.

Criteria were identified in the results. For instance the lazy loading and the attachment of security updates to functional updates are of utmost importance for our experts to make a software more sustainable. The criteria found in the questionnaire are indicated in Table 1 with the percentage of respondents who identified them in their answers.

The last two questions were open-ended for developers to see if they were aware of ways to assess sustainability. These answers show that developers are not familiar with the right design and development techniques, nor the ways software damages hardware. In addition, some companies do not consider design and sustainability in their strategies.

**Table 1.** Identified criteria

| Criteria | State of art | Interviews | Quest |
|---|---|---|---|
| Separation between security updates and functional updates | | | 52,2% |
| Lazy loading | | X | 52,2% |
| Object oriented vs Functional programming | | X | |
| Cloud synchronization | [8, 24, 25] | X | |
| Database vs File | [7] | X | |
| Local vs Network storage | [7] | X | |
| Network call | [7] | X | |
| Compiled vs Interpreted | [21] | X | |
| Background work | [21] | | 47,8% |
| Automatically launch on default startup | | | 39,1% |

(*continued*)

**Table 1.** (*continued*)

| Criteria | State of art | Interviews | Quest |
|---|---|---|---|
| Night/Day mode | | X | 43,5% |
| Optimize the use of the CPU | [21] | | 39,1% |
| Optimizing algorithms (Human action) | [23] | X | |
| Optimize code instructions (Compiler action) | [23] | X | |
| I/O RAM vs Hard drive rate | [8, 26] | X | |
| Optimizing the use of the memory | [8] | | 21,7% |
| Binary that takes up space | | X | 4,3% |
| Percentage of use of open source | [27, 7] | | 13% |
| Bugs | | | 20% |
| The poor legibility of the code to better understand it (Evolution correction) | | X | |

# 4  Sustainability Matrix

We defined a matrix where the software score identifies the sustainability degree of a mobile application (From 1 for a bad sustainability to 5, for an excellent one). Each criteria is a characteristic of either the design phase or the development phase. They are associated to a weight identified by their appearance in the literature, the interviews and the questionnaire. This matrix could also be used for any other kind of software with slight adjustments (on criteria and on weights).

## 4.1  Eleven Design Sustainability Criteria

**Separation Between Security Updates and Functional Updates (Weight: 30).** Partial updates require significantly less energy for all technologies [28]. It is then useful to identify which kind of updates are strictly necessary. The software publisher must be transparent in separating updates by giving the customer the choice of accepting security updates (essential) and accepting or refuting functional updates (facultative).

**Lazy Loading (Weight: 15).** In a Web application, data retrieval of other services is sometimes slow. Thus, users may feel that the website is slow if the web page is deployed only after the data is fully processed. Nevertheless, using Lazy Loading allows the page to render and defer only a small portion until the request is ready, pushes the complete content at a later date [29]. This happens in order to provide a better user experience but it also decreases the energy consumption at run-time. Lazy loading is a design model that initializes an object only when it becomes necessary. In this way, Lazy Loading actually contributes to the efficiency of the operation of the software if it is used in a correct and adequate way. This makes Lazy Loading an ideal property where network content is accessible and the initialization time has to be reduced, as in the case of web pages.

**Object Oriented vs Functional Programming (Weight: 10).** According to our experts, object-oriented programming is lighter and faster than functional programming since it uses only the objects needed to perform the expected functions. This limits the use of material resources to a minimum. As a matter of fact, in object oriented programming, the modeling step is of great importance, since the transcription of real elements in virtual form takes place during this step. In functional programming, all elements are defined as functions and the code runs through successive calls of functions.

**Cloud Synchronization (Weight: 9).** Companies use the cloud to store their data and enable their employers to work remotely. This therefore requires a sharp increase in hardware requirements to back up data, usually accompanied by high expectations in terms of security, which translates into an oversized physical infrastructure. However, studies begin to appear on the sustainability of cloud use, as [25] that shows that cloud ERP services have a positive impact on the environmental performance of an organization by reducing data losses, and that real-time cloud operations improve processing time and reduce the misuse of resources. The criteria weight is then susceptible to evolve.

**Database vs File (Weight: 9).** The software structure of files is simple. However, the software structure of database is more complicated and robust. Thus, and in order to use less energy in order to preserve the environment, the software structure of the database must be simple and organized in such a way as to facilitate queries.

**Local vs Network Storage (Weight: 9).** It identifies what type of storage is used. Network storage requires a network to store data in data centers. Data centers requires constant energy and cooling, which increases the negative environmental impact. Local storage stores data directly in memory, so it uses only part of the energy needed to operate. It can also be turned off, which reduces the negative environmental impact.

**Network Call (Weight: 5).** This criterion indicates the number of requests that the software has submitted. Higher the number of requests, greater the impact of the software on the environment across the hardware and network.

**Compiled vs Interpreted (Weight: 5).** This criterion indicates the type of programming language used: Compiled or Interpreted. Compiled language is faster and translates the code directly into machine language, while interpreted language needs an interpreter, which complicates the procedure and consumes more energy. Thus, compiled language is more favorable in support for environmental requirements.

**Background Work (Weight: 4).** This criterion indicates whether the software contains components that work in the background, that is, whether the software works when it is not used by the user. Indeed, such software consumes energy, even if it is in an inactive case. This announces that this criterion makes the software less Green.

**Automatically Launch on Default Startup (Weight: 2).** This criterion means that software dependencies work directly by default at boot time. Therefore, this software consumes energy and hardware components, although they are not used at the user's request.

**Night/Day Mode (Weight: 2).** According to experts, night mode has proven to be less energy-intensive. Thus, its use prolongs the life of the battery.

### 4.2 Nine Development Sustainability Criteria

**Optimize the Use of the CPU (Weight: 40).** This criterion indicates the number of accesses to the CPU. The higher the number of accesses to the CPU, the greater the power consumption, and the shorter the life of the CPU. [30] proposes a model for determining a frequency level that minimizes energy consumption during parallel application execution (with an energy saving of 7% for NAS benchmarks).

**Optimizing Algorithms (Human Action) (Weight: 14).** It means that developers have improved already existing algorithms, to improve their performance by making them more sober. The aim is to reduce the use of hardware resources and energy consumption.

**Optimize Code Instructions (Compiler Action) (Weight: 10).** This criterion determines whether the compiler, by improving the algorithm without the need for developer intervention, makes the software execution procedure greener.

**I/O RAM vs Hard Drive Rate (Weight: 10).** This criterion indicates the number of accesses to the RAM and hard disk. After consulting the experts, it appeared that the hard disk consumes more energy than the RAM, which makes the optimization of the use of the hard disk favorable to the protection of the environment.

**Optimizing the Use of the Memory (Weight: 5).** It stresses the importance of the sobriety of the algorithms and the way the software was programmed, in order to preserve the environment. The simpler and more efficient the algorithms and the programming way, the less the software needs access to memory, and the less energy it consumes.

**Binary that Takes Up Space (Weight: 5).** The design should focus on the needs to avoid making the software "obese". The latter will take up a lot of space if it embeds unnecessary code. Thus, the software will use more hardware resources with no real benefit to the user. This surplus will take more binary space than the one imagined in the design phase, and it will consume more of the smartphone's hardware resources. We can say that this way of planning a software with a surplus of features contributes to the programmed obsolescence, and causes the premature renewal of the smartphone.

**Percentage of Use of Open Source (Weight: 4).** Its advantage lies in the ability of users to use the software without being dependent on the editor and its updates. These updates often render old computer devices obsolete, which requires purchase of new ones. The ability of users to use, improve, and modify open-source software allows them to extend the life of their computer devices, thereby protecting the environment.

**Bugs (Weight: 4).** This criterion means that the software has a lot of bugs, and if it requires regular maintenance. In this case, the software must be updated regularly. This makes the software more obese, therefore more obsolete.

**The Poor Legibility of the Code to Better Understand it (Evolution Correction) (Weight: 4).** This criterion means that the software is well developed, and the code well written and clear. This facilitates development by developers and execution by the compiler.

## 5   Evaluation

In order to validate the matrix, a practical case concerning the "Éco2mix" mobile software, developed by the company RTE, was studied. This application is accessible to everyone, not just RTE customers or its agents. Éco2mix is operable on Android and IOS. This application is dedicated to exposing RTE data on energy uses and production (nuclear, solar, hydraulic, photovoltaic, etc.) both throughout France and at the level of administrative regions and in certain metropolitan areas. The application also gives the average energy consumption of a house in France and the possibility to compare it with those of individuals. Its objective is to better manage the energy balance. Trade in all electrical parameters at the level of the French regions and between France and its neighboring countries has also been included in this application.

**Matrix Construction.** We interviewed the project manager of this application development and filled the sustainability matrix with him (cf. Figure 2) to help him make his auto-evaluation. Next step is to calculate the score of the application based on the matrix results. Calculus of category score is made on the following way. (a) Each level is multiplied by its weight. (b) The sum of all results is done for the category and modified to represent the percentage of sustainability. Here, for the design, the sum of all weighted criteria is 279. Its rate over 500 (the maximum score) gives 55,8%, an average score. And the development category gives a rate of 76,875%, which is quite good.

**Results Evaluation.** We discussed these results with the project manager who recognized the results as true for this application. From a sustainability point of view, Éco2mix is a good software both in the design aspect and in the development aspect. Moreover, this interview allowed the project manager to identify some improvement for the future to improve the software sustainability, as follows. (a) It would be good for Éco2mix to make the separation between security updates and functional updates and to let the client free to choose the type of update to install. (b) Developers have every interest in reducing the number of requests with the network, in order to optimize the environmental performance of Éco2mix. (c) The energy performance of Éco2mix is affected by the lack of night/day mode, so it seemed useful to treat this aspect in order to improve the performance. (d) It appeared that open-source development is more suitable for the sustainability of software, by facilitating the maintenance, modification and improvement of the code at the level of security as well as functional. (e) Developers will be encouraged to optimize the Eco2mix code in order to have fewer bugs, which will increase its environmental performance. (f) The code is written in a rather complicated way, which reinforces the interest of making it easier to read, modify and improve.

The project manager found the test useful, as it allowed him to identify the elements that make up sustainability of software, elements that seem relevant to him and that he will use in his next projects.

| Conception Criteria | Weight | 1 | 2 | 3 | 4 | 5 | Explanation |
|---|---|---|---|---|---|---|---|
| Separation between security updates & functional updates | 30 | X | | | | | Eco2mix is often supported by functional updates, and is not always supported by security updates. Eco2mix does not separate the two types of updates. |
| Lazy loading | 15 | | | X | | | Eco2mix interacts with the user based on data already downloaded at the start. Then, as it happens, Eco2mix downloads the necessary data for the operations performed by the user. |
| Object Oriented vs Functional Programming | 10 | | | | X | | Developers mainly used Object Oriented Programming. |
| Cloud Synchronization | 9 | | | | | X | The cloud is not part of the technical specifications of Eco2mix. |
| Database VS file | 9 | | | X | | | Eco2mix data are organized in both Files and Database. |
| Local VS Network Storage | 9 | | | | | X | Eco2mix stores its data locally, which gives it the right value. |
| Network Call | 5 | | X | | | | Eco2mix does a lot of queries with the network, which decreases the assigned value. |
| Compiled VS Interpreted | 5 | | | X | | | Eco2mix is coded in Java (Compiled), PHP (interpreted) and JavaScript (interpreted). |
| Background work | 4 | | | | | X | Eco2mix does not work on background (except few processes such as the notification process). |
| Automatically launch on default startup | 2 | | X | | | | Eco2mix starts automatically at startup, in order to perform some tasks. |
| Night/Day Mode | 2 | X | | | | | Eco2mix does not support the feature of night/day mode. |
| **Development Criteria** | | | | | | | |
| Optimize the use of the CPU | 40 | | | | X | | Eco2mix does not use the CPU very much. |
| Optimizing Algorithms (Human Action) | 14 | | | | | X | Eco2mix is rather front-end software, so there are not many algorithms to optimize. |
| Optimize code instructions (Compiler action) | 10 | | | X | | | The developers of Eco2mix do not use compiler optimization. |
| I/O RAM VS Hard Drive Rate | 10 | | | | X | | Eco2mix is mobile and web software, it does not use Hard Drive, and it occupies only a small part of the RAM. |
| Optimizing Memory use | 5 | | | | X | | Eco2mix does not use a lot of memory. |
| Binary that takes up space | 5 | | | | | X | Eco2mix is a largely lightweight software, so its binary space is 50MB. |
| Percentage Open Source use | 4 | | X | | | | Eco2mix is developed in closed-source. |
| Bugs | 4 | | X | | | | Eco2mix often suffers from Bugs. |
| The poor legibility of the code to better understand it (Evolution correction) | 4 | | | X | | | The Eco2mix code is a bit complicated. |

**Fig. 2.** Eco2mix sustainability matrix

# 6  Conclusion

We developed a matrix for project managers to test the sustainability of their software. This matrix was based on the results of a literature study, interviews with experts and a questionnaire published on the web on professional networks. This questionnaire contained two types of criteria: positive and negative, making the software more or less durable. We evaluated the sustainability matrix on a smartphone application and discussed the results with the application project manager.

The criteria of the matrix were assembled theoretically on the basis of the results of the interviews and questionnaire, as well as the literature. However, it is preferable for future work to benefit from measurement equipment in order to truly assess the relevance of these criteria and their impact on software sustainability. Each criterion should be tested separately. As mentioned earlier, at this stage there are only sustainability testing tools dedicated to websites. It will therefore be necessary to build sustainability testing tools for software implemented on all computer devices, such as smartphones and computers.

The matrix forms a good basis for evaluating the durability of software. It has been divided into four categories: Design, Development, Use and Integration. The work presented here covered the first two categories, while the next two categories will be the subject of further interesting work. We also plan to use the extended matrix on several other cases to test its efficiency.

# References

1. Munasinghe Institute for Development (MIND). Integrating sustainable development and climate change in the IPCC fourth assessment report. IPCC Expert Meeting (2003)
2. Orgerie, A-C.: L'informatique émet plus de gaz à effet de serre que l'aviation. Pour la Science journal, n° 457 (2015)
3. Brauer, B., Eisel, M., Kolbe, L.M.: The state of the art in smart city research – a literature analysis on green is solutions to foster environmental sustainability. In: Pacific Asia Conference on Information Systems (PACIS) (2015)
4. vom Brocke, J., Loos, P., Seidel, S., Watson, R.T.: Green IS. Bus. Inf. Syst. Eng. 5(5), 295–297 (2013). https://doi.org/10.1007/s12599-013-0288-y
5. Maurey, H., Chaize, P., Chevrollier, G., Houllegatte, J-M.: Rapport d'information fait au nom de la commission de l'aménagement du territoire et du développement durable par la mission d'information sur l'empreinte environnementale du numérique. Sénat. Report N° 555 (2020)
6. Byung-Chul, C., Hang-Sik, S., Su-Yol, L, Tak, H.: Life cycle assessment of a personal computer and its effective recycling rate. Int. J. Life Cycle Assess. 11(2), 122–128 (2006)
7. Mobbs, P.: A practical guide to sustainable IT. Commissioned by the Association for Progressive Communications (APC) (2012)
8. Ardito, L., Morisio, M.: Green IT – available data and guidelines for reducing energy consumption in IT systems. Sustain. Comput. Inf. Syst. 4(1) 24–32 (2014)
9. Warren-Myers, G.: The value of sustainability in real estate: a review from a valuation perpective. J. Property Invest. Finan. 30(2), 115–144 (2012)
10. Kelly, G.: Sustainability at home: policy measures for energy-efficient applicances. Renew. Sustain. Energy Rev. 16(9), 6851–6860 (2012)
11. Jones, P., Clarke-Hill, C., Comfort, D., Hillier, D.: Marketing and sustainability. J. Market. Intell. Plan. 26(2), 123–130 (2008)

12. Dobranskyte-Niskota, A., Perrujo, A., Jesinghauss, J., Jensen, P.: Indicators to assess sustainability of transport activities. JRC Scientific and Technical Reports (2009)
13. Dao, V., Langella, I., Carbo, J.: From green to sustainability: information technology and an integrated sustainability framework. J. Strategic Inf. Syst. 20(1), 63–79 (2011)
14. Loeser, F.: Green IT and green is: definition of constructs and overview of current practices. In: 19th Americas Conference on Information Systems (AMCIS) (2013)
15. Murugesan, S.: Harnessing Green IT: Principles and Practices. IT Prof. 10(1), 24–33 (2008)
16. Bordage, F.: Environmental footprint of the digital world. GreenIT (2019)
17. Naumann, S., Dick, M., Kern, E., Johann, T.: The greensoft model: a reference model for green and sustainable software and its engineering. Sustain. Comput. Inf. Syst. 1(4), 294–304 (2011)
18. Colapinto, C., Jayaraman, R., Ben Abdelaziz, F., La Torre, D.: Environmental sustainability and multifaceted development: multi-criteria decision models with applications. Ann. Oper. Res. 293(2), 405–432 (2019). https://doi.org/10.1007/s10479-019-03403-y
19. Jamwal, A., Agrawal, R., Sharma, M., Kumar, V.: Review on multi-criteria decision analysis in sustainable manufacturing decision making. Int. J. Sustain. Eng. 14(3), 202–225 (2020)
20. Brauer, B., Ebermann, C., Hildebrandt, B., Remané, G., Kolbe, L.: Green by app: the contribution of mobile applications to environmental sustainability. PACIS 2016, 220 (2016)
21. Pang, C., Hindle, A., Adams, B., Hassan, A.: What do programmers know about software energy consumption? IEEE Xplore 33(3), 83–89 (2015)
22. Caroll, A., Heiser, G.: An analysis of power consumption in a smartphone. In: USENIX Conference on USENIX Annual Technical Conference (2010)
23. Deneckère, R., Rubio, G.: EcoSoft: Proposition of an eco-label for software sustainability. In: Dupuy-Chessa, S., Proper, H. (eds.) Advanced Information Systems Engineering Workshops. CAiSE 2020. Lecture Notes in Business Information Processing, vol. 382, pp. 121–132. Springer, Cham (2020). https://doi.org/10.1007/978-3-030-49165-9_11
24. Accenture, Cloud Computing and Sustainability: The Environmental Benefits of Moving to the Cloud, Accenture Whitepaper (2010)
25. Gupta, S., Meissonier, R., Drave, V.A., Roubaud, D.: Examining the impact of cloud ERP on sustainable performance: a dynamic capability view. Int. J. Inf. Manage. 51, 102028 (2020)
26. Larsson P.: Energy-Efficient Software Guidelines, p. 14 (2011)
27. Chang, V., Mills, H., Newhouse, S.: From open source to long-term sustainability: review of business models and case studies. In: Proceedings of the UK e-Science All Hands Meeting 2007 (2007)
28. Ruckebusch, P., Giannoulis, S., Moerman, I., Hoebeke, J., De Poorter, E.: Modelling the energy consumption for over-the-air software updates in LPWAN networks: SigFox, LoRa and IEEE 802.15.4g. Internet of Things 3–4, 104–119 (2018)
29. del Pilar Salas-Zárate, M., Alor-Hernández, G., Valencia-García, R., Rodríguez-Mazahua, L., Rodríguez-González, A., López Cuadrado, J.L.: Analyzing best practices on web development frameworks: the lift approach. Sci. Comput. Prog. 102, 1–19 (2015)
30. Sundriyal, V., Sosonkina, M.: Modeling of the CPU frequency to minimize energy consumption in parallel applications. Sustain. Comput. Inf. Syst. 17, 1–8 (2018)

# Representing Habits as Streams of Situational Contexts

Xiaoyue Li$^{(\boxtimes)}$ (ID), Marcelo Rodas-Britez (ID), Matteo Busso (ID), and Fausto Giunchiglia (ID)

Department of Information Engineering and Computer Science, University of Trento, Trento, Italy
{xiaoyue.li,marcelo.rodasbritez,matteo.busso,
fausto.giunchiglia}@unitn.it

**Abstract.** The increasing use of smart devices allows us to extract massive streams of data, e.g., sensor streams, questionnaires, answers, annotations, etc. This information is crucial for the recognition of people's behaviours and habits. The main challenge is how to represent and organize such large scale, complex and heterogeneous data streams. This representation should allow for the management of all possible and unpredictable personal situations. The main goal of this paper is to propose a formalization of the personal situational context, showing how it can model real-life situations. The intuition is that, by collecting data from different people, we can populate the model and enhance the knowledge about those people by learning different aspects of their life habits. We start defining the abstract notions of the personal situational context and habits. Then, we provide an informal representation of such notions. Finally, we generate a universal ontological model of the situation context and habits, formally represented with an Entity Type Graph.

**Keywords:** Representing habits · Situational context · Data streams

## 1 Introduction

Habits[1] are "behavioral patterns acquired by frequent repetition or physiologic exposure that show themselves in regularity or increased facility of performance." A habit is regular, predictable, learned by practice and is performed almost automatically [1]. Knowing about habits can help predict people's activities, thus supporting them in everyday life. But how to learn about them? Smart devices can collect a large amount of personal data, e.g., answers to questionnaires, annotations, and sensors. For instance, a study used smartphone data (call records,

---

[1] https://www.merriam-webster.com/dictionary/habit.

Xiaoyue receives funding from the China Scholarships Council (No. 202107820014). Marcelo, Fausto and Matteo receive funding from the project "DELPhi - DiscovEring Life Patterns" funded by the MIUR (PRIN) 2017.

J. Horkoff et al. (Eds.): CAiSE 2022, LNBIP 451, pp. 86–92, 2022.
https://doi.org/10.1007/978-3-031-07478-3_7

Bluetooth logs, and others) to study students' social networks and daily activities [2]. The StudentLife project [3] employs smartphone sensors and answers to questionnaires to infer students' mental health, academic performance, and so on. These are examples of studies that used smart devices streams to study partial aspects of people's habits, but the challenge of formalizing a universal ontological model still remains.

Context is a theory that describes the world from an individual's perspective [4,5]. Situational contexts are very powerful means for modeling the user's life, as understood by the users themselves [6]. As such, they provide a powerful means for organizing a large amount of highly heterogeneous data streams that are needed to represent possible daily situations and, as a particular case, personal habits. Some work in this direction is described in [5], where contexts are used to provide a unified account of people, devices, the environment and services provided. Further, the work in [7] models the personal context and uses it to represent different dimensions, e.g., the spatial-temporal and the social dimension.

This paper improves on the previous work by extending our notion of situational context, by introducing the notion of habits, and by defining a general formal model in the form of an Entity Type Graph (ETG). This ETG allows us to organize and store large amounts of data streams. In the ETG, nodes are the entities of our model (e.g., Person, Location), and links represent the relations existing across entities (e.g., With relation between Object and Sub-event).

We will exemplify our notions, across the paper, via the following *motivating example*. Mary usually shops with her smartphone and Bob in the Sun market. They talk with each other in the shopping. Often, Mary studies in office A with her laptop. After that, Mary studies with her laptop on the balcony of her home and then has dinner with Bob in the kitchen. All the above activities are habits, happening at different frequencies. For instance, shopping at the Sun market happens every week, while Mary goes to work every weekday.

## 2 Modeling Life Sequences, Contexts and Habits

A situational context represents a real life scenario from the perspective of a person, that we call me, e.g., Mary in the example. We call the *Life sequence* a sequence of contexts during a certain period of time. We have the following:

$$S(me) = \langle C_1(me), \ldots, C_n(me) \rangle; \quad 1 \leq i \leq n \tag{1}$$

where $C_i(me)$ is the $i_{th}$ situational context of me. We assume that me is involved in only one personal context at a time. In fact, at any given moment, a person can be in only one place. Hence, $S$ is a sequence of contexts of me covering the full period under consideration, where contexts without overlapping. In turn, we model the situational context of me $C(me)$ by me's views as follows:

$$C(me) = \langle L(C(me)), E(L(C(me))) \rangle \tag{2}$$

In the following, we simplify the notation by dropping the argument me when no ambiguity arises. $L(C)$ is the *Location* of me. The location defines the spatial boundaries inside which the current scenario evolves. $E(L(C))$ is the *Event* within which me is involved at the moment. The current event defines the temporal boundaries within which the current context evolves. An event is parameterized on the location as we may have different events occurring in the same location. Location and event are the priors of experience, defining the scenario that needs to be modeled. They univocally define the spatio-temporal coordinates of any person in the world. The change of context coincides with a change of the current location or of the current event. For Mary's shopping example, the location *Sun market* and the event *shopping* give an example of the (current) context at a certain moment in time.

Inside a certain context, me can be inside one or more locations, which change any time me moves from one place to another. For example, when at home, Mary may stay on the balcony or in the kitchen. We have the following:

$$L(C) = \langle L_1(C), \dots, L_n(C) \rangle; \quad 1 \le i \le n \tag{3}$$

where $L_i(C)$ is a spatial part of $L(C)$. We say that $L_i(C)$ is a *sub-location* of $L(C)$. If me is in one location, we say that the current context is *static*, and we have that $L(C) = L_1(C) = \dots = L_n(C)$. Otherwise, we say that the current context is *dynamic*. In the above example, Mary's home (i.e., $L(C)$) contains the balcony (i.e., $L_1(C)$) and the kitchen (i.e., $L_2(C)$). Depending on the level of detail at which we represent Mary's life, we may have a static context, i.e., Mary being at home, or a dynamic context, i.e., Mary being first on the balcony and then in the kitchen. The choice is part of the way Mary thinks of what she is doing, see, e.g., [8] for more details on the issue of the subjectivity of (the descriptions of) the situational contexts. Within contexts, events behave as contexts within life sequences. We have the following:

$$E(L(C)) = \langle E_1(L(C)), \dots, E_n(L(C)) \rangle; \quad 1 \le i \le n \tag{4}$$

with $E_i(L(C))$ part of $E(L(C))$. Similarly to the above, we say that any $E_i(L(C))$ is a *sub-event* of $E(L(C))$. Sub-events may be parallel or sequential or mixed. We may again have that $E(L(C)) = E(L_1(C)) = \dots = E(L_n(C))$. In fact, with static contexts, events are distinct (while occurring within the same location), while in dynamic contexts we may have, but not necessarily, the same event occurring in different locations. Thus, for instance, at home, Mary will usually do different things, e.g., cooking and watching TV, while she might keep talking when moving from one place to another. In this case, we say that the current life sequence is *location-dynamic* but *event-static*. The case of *traveling* is of particular relevance. Assume, for instance, that Mary will be traveling from Trento to Rome and that she will be doing many different things while traveling. This real world event will be modeled as a static context if the location considered is Italy, or as a life sequence of length greater than one if the different locations touched by the trip, e.g., Trento, Rome, are explicitly represented.

The context defined by location and event will contain, within its spatio-temporal boundaries, various types of general objects interacting among them. It is required that me is one of them. We capture this intuition by defining the notion of *Context Part P(C)* defined as follows:

$$P(C) = \langle me, \{P\}, \{O\}, \{A\} \rangle \qquad (5)$$

where $\{P\}$, $\{O\}$ and $\{A\}$ are, respectively, a set of persons (e.g., Bob), a set of objects (e.g., a smartphone) and a set of actions involving them. As from Definition 5, even within the same location and the same event, the world evolves, because of actions. For instance, in the shopping scenario, the event *shopping* involves Mary's action "speak to Bob" and Bob's action "speak to Mary". We say that a context is a *static context* when there are no changes. Data streams in fact capture the instantaneous properties of static contexts. Given the above definitions, we define Habits $H$ as follows:

$$H = \langle S_{a_1} : a_1, \ldots, S_{a_n} : a_n, F \rangle; \quad 1 \leq i \leq n \qquad (6)$$

where $S_i$ is a life sequence and $a_i$ is an *activity* involving me involving any other element in the current context. Examples of $a_i$ are: *being in a location, being involved in an event, being together with a person, using an object, performing an action*. $F$ is the *Frequency* at which $H$ occurs. There are various levels of flexibility which can be used in the definition of $F$, but this is out of the scope of this short paper. We have therefore five basic types of habits: spatial habits, temporal habits, social habits, material habits, and action habits. An example of habit is Mary's material habit of always carrying her smartphone and laptop.

## 3    Representing Life Sequences, Contexts and Habits

Figure 1 is an example of informal representation of life sequence (see Definition 1), as described in the motivating example. A life sequence is represented as a sequence of contexts, where, for each context, we draw location, event, me, person and object with boxes. Events and actions are drawn with green borders. For each context, the most external reference is the location container, which may contain multiple sub-locations. Multiple locations are ordered from the top to the bottom according to time. Each location contains an event, which may contain multiple sub-events. Multiple sub-events are ordered from the top to the end by their happening time. For example, in the bottom box of Fig. 1, the location is Mary's home, which contains the balcony and kitchen. At Mary's home, we have the default event *being at home*. An event box contains me, person and object boxes, e.g., Mary (me), Mary's smartphone box in the top box.

As from Definition 6, habits are just sequences of life sequences where specific activities have been selected annotated by the frequency at which they occur. This means that Fig. 1 can be used to represent habits simply by selecting the relevant actions, as from Definition 6 (see the comment after Definition 6). Thus,

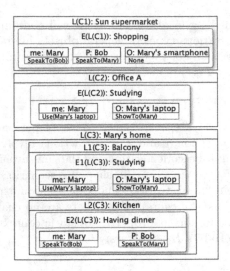

**Fig. 1.** The contexts of mary.

for instance, the life sequence in Fig. 1 can be used to define and represent the following spatial habit

$$H_S = \langle \langle C1 \rangle : Sunmarket, 1\,week \rangle$$

where we have assumed that $\langle\,C1\,\rangle$ is a life sequence containing the single context C1 and that the habit $H_S$ occurs every week.

The key observation, which allows for the representation life sequences of any length and representing any possible real world situation, is that contexts can be represented as ETGs where location and event define the spatio-temporal boundaries within which such models hold. Figure 2 reports the corresponding ETG, where for simplicity, we have not represented actions. (They would be modeled as properties of entities.)

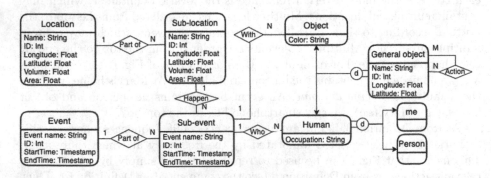

**Fig. 2.** The ETG modeling the situational context.

From the definition of $C_i(me)$, we represent five main entities. Based on this, we have the following entity types: General Object, Object, Human (Person and me), Location, and Event, drawn with nodes in ETG.

1. General Object: Represent any object in any context.
2. Object: Extend from General Object and represent the non-human objects in any context (e.g., Smartphone).
3. Human: Extend from General Object and represent humans (e.g., me, Person).
4. Location: Represent any Location. Sub-location is a part of Location.
5. Event: Represent any Event. Sub-event is a part of Event.

We add the properties with data types of entity types in nodes, e.g., Name: String in the Location node. We show relations among entity types with rhombuses. For example, we have two Relations: With and Who, the first linking events with objects, the second linking events with humans. These two relations implement Definition 5. There are inheritance relations among entity types. We use the "d" in a circle that connects the superclass with a double line and each subclass using a single line with an arrow. For example, the superclass General object has two subclasses Object and Human.

Our graph representations will allow us to create, read, update, and relate information as they are recognized. This model, in a preliminary version, has been validated by using it in a large scale data collection and study experiment in the SmartUniversity (SU) project. This project used the iLog app [9] to collect one hundred and eighty-four students' daily life data over a period of four weeks. We have two studies that used this data collection [8,10]. Mapping data collections into our model opens the possibility of learning people's habits.

## 4 Conclusion

This paper proposes a general model of life sequences, situational contexts and habits. The (sequence of) ETG model(s) defined based on these definitions can be used to organize large scale data streams, as they can be collected by the sensors of smartphones and smartwatches.

## References

1. Rogers, J.C.: Habits: do we practice what we preach? Occup. Ther. J. Res. **20**(1 suppl), 119S–122S (2000)
2. Eagle, N., Pentland, A.S.: Reality mining: sensing complex social systems. Pers. Ubiquit. Comput. **10**(4), 255–268 (2006). https://doi.org/10.1007/s00779-005-0046-3
3. Wang, R., et al.: Studentlife: assessing mental health, academic performance and behavioral trends of college students using smartphones. In: Proceedings of ACM - UBICOMP, pp. 3–14 (2014)

4. Giunchiglia, F., Bignotti, E., Zeni, M.: Personal context modelling and annotation. In: 2017 IEEE International Conference on Pervasive Computing and Communications Workshops (PerCom Workshops), pp. 117–122. IEEE (2017)
5. Hervás, R., Bravo, J., Fontecha, J.: A context model based on ontological languages: a proposal for information visualization. J. Univ. C.S. **16**(12), 1539–1555 (2010)
6. Bouquet, P., Giunchiglia, E., Giunchiglia, F.: Contexts, locality and generality. Mathware Soft. Comput. **3**(1[-2]), 47–57 (1996)
7. Giunchiglia, F., Britez, M.R., Bontempelli, A., Li, X.: Streaming and learning the personal context. In: Twelfth International Workshop Modelling and Reasoning in Context, p. 19 (2021)
8. Zhang, W., et al.: Putting human behavior predictability in context. EPJ Data Sci. **10**(1), 1–22 (2021). https://doi.org/10.1140/epjds/s13688-021-00299-2
9. Zeni, M., Zaihrayeu, I., Giunchiglia, F.: Multi-device activity logging. In: Proceedings of ACM - UBICOMP: Adjunct Publication, pp. 299–302 (2014)
10. Zeni, M., Zhang, W., Bignotti, E., Passerini, A., Giunchiglia, F.: Fixing mislabeling by human annotators leveraging conflict resolution and prior knowledge. ACM UBICOMP **3**(1), 32 (2019)

# Robots and Choreography: A Contribution to Artificial Sentience Characterization

Micheline Lelièvre[1], Robin Zebrowski[2], and Eric Gressier Soudan[3(✉)]

[1] PIGNON SUR RUE, 75009 Paris, France
`micheline@micheline.net`
[2] Cognitive Science, Beloit College, Beloit, WI 53511, USA
`zebrowsr@beloit.edu`
[3] CEDRIC Lab, CNAM, Paris, France
`eric.gressier_soudan@cnam.fr`

**Abstract.** The research work presented in this paper is at an early stage. While tests for artificial intelligence/consciousness/sentience continue to evolve, there still doesn't seem to be any consensus on what exactly we hope to capture with such tests. In this paper, we explore the possibility of an arts-based performative test for machine sentience. We analyzed a specific choreography, called Chemins à coulisses, through both the language and experience of the choreographer and a spectator, and we offer some additional theoretical lenses through which to tackle this problem, including phenomenology and distributed systems. We offer the beginnings of an approach to creating a performance-based test where the machine doesn't merely imitate steps but engages in a meaningful way with performers and spectators. There may be an under explored area for benchmarking machine sentience that sits at the intersection of phenomenology, choreography, and distributed systems.

**Keywords:** Machine sentience · Choreography · Inter-subjectivity · Distributed systems

## 1 Introduction

We wanted to address Smart Life through the robots perspective. Robots will be part of our future to face incoming challenge of humanity. The new generation of robots will be smarter and able to interact accurately with human beings as we can see it in movies, novels or series. From our point of view robots will be enhanced through machine consciousness [1]. In the field of machine consciousness we are interested on a subfield called machine sentience, or artificial sentience.

Sentience is defined as an ability "of experiencing an affective state" [2]. It can define human-animal and human-human communications. Our belief is that sentience will be extended to human-robot communications in a close future [25]. We can imagine teamwork between humans and robots crafting complex building on a remote and dangerous planet far from the solar system.

J. Horkoff et al. (Eds.): CAiSE 2022, LNBIP 451, pp. 93–102, 2022.
https://doi.org/10.1007/978-3-031-07478-3_8

As sentience is coming into play, we need to evaluate the ability of any robot to deliver it. Artificial Intelligence testing emerged from A. Turing works [3]. The idea of defining Sentience Testing has been introduced in [4]. This proposal was disruptive but needed a missing point of view: cognitive and philosophical sciences [4].

This paper describes a preliminary work on artificial testing. The second section describes robots as part of our culture and how they are imagined as part of our future. Section 3 provides an analysis of a choreography that could help to design artificial sentience testing. Section 4 regroups the point of view of the three authors about addressing artificial sentience testing through a dance performance. Section 5 provides some preliminary hints about artificial sentience testing. Section 6 concludes the paper.

## 2  Robots as Part of an Imagined Future of Humanity

Since the early 20th century, robots have played a prominent role in our images of the future. From books to movies, comics and TV series, there have been many robots that help us think about our future with them around us, from Maria of the Metropolis movie in 1927 by Fritz Lang, to the very popular R2D2 of the movie Star Wars in 1977 by G. Lucas, or the peaceful CHAPIE of the movie from N. Blomkamp and T. Tatchell in 2015. From HAL of the movie 2001: A space Odyssey in 1968 by Arthur C. Clarke, and S. Kubrik to HER of the movie by S. Jonze in 2013, robots have always challenged our mind and our way of thinking.

The movie A.I. Artificial Intelligence of S. Spielberg in 2001 shows how intelligence and emotions can help to get robots to be more human-like, and potentially to be the species that survives the future. One may notice that emotion and empathy are at the heart of various AI TV series: for example, we can watch Lost in Space, season 2 on Netflix, December 2019, where a teenager, Will Robinson, is tightly emotionally connected to an alien robot he saved. More unexpectedly, in Better than Us on Netflix, August 2019, episode 5, the robot of the family, Arisa, a very new generation of robots, explains to Safronov, the father, that she is able to sense emotional states from humans. This line of possibility from fiction mirrors V. Gal's real PhD thesis work in the same area [5]. Sometimes in fiction robots act together, as swarms or in collaborative teams, like Gorgonides vs Commando Elite in the movie Small Soldiers 1998 from J. Dante, or Autonomous Mobile Swords in the movie Screamers from C. Duguay 1995, and generally it turns bad, as the robots turn against their creators like Terminators do in the movie The Terminator, from J. Cameron, 1984. While our science fiction often shows us the limits and possibilities of our imaginations, robots, and especially swarms of robots, are part of our future and require careful attention.

Swarms of robots have also their own benchmarks. The RoboCup, where two teams of autonomous NAOs from SoftBank Robotics play soccer against each other, offers yet another benchmark for ongoing robotics research. The aim of this challenge is to defeat a professional world champion soccer team around 2050 [6]. Movies can again show a different perspective about how we can measure and test the possibility of robot intelligence and/or sentience. For example, biological androids, known as replicants in the movie Blade Runner[1] from R. Scott, 1982, are detected by the Voight-Kampff test. The Voight-Kampff test evaluates the emotional response to an aggressive questionnaire and measures the empathy level of the tested. In the movie, it is supposed to be the dysfunctional emotional response that reveals the replicants to be different than the humans they resemble. The film challenges this very relevant capacity. It is also interesting to mention, the Baseline Test from the movie Blade Runner 2049 by D. Villeneuve, 2017, it is a "more advanced technology" that focuses on Replicant operational stability. Operational stability could be associated to some kind of alexithymia. Emotions, free will and consciousness are at the heart of the future of robots and humankind.

Humans have always been keen on comparing computers against human intelligence. Alan Turing defined the first AI test in 1950 [3]. Deep Blue defeated the chess world champion Garry Kasparov for the first time in 1997. It was one of the greatest benchmarks of AI research progress. Since then, benchmarking of AI has never stopped. Google's DeepMind AI won against Lee Sedol, one of the world top players of Go, in 2016. But AI has become affordable to developers. There is an AI based painter trained with Vincent Van Gogh paintings and landscape pictures known as VincentGanGogh [7]. It is able to transform a photo by adopting Van Gogh painting style and to post it on Instagram. VincentGanGogh writes hashtags, poems inspired by the painting it provided. It "like"'s photos from other artists, and sometimes comments on them. Some people do not notice that it is not a human being. VincentGanGogh is a serverless program using Generative Adversarial Networks (a type of neural networks) based on AI Azure services. VincentGanGogh shows how Arts come into play with AI in a very convincing manner. It demonstrated that there can be compelling arts-based tests and benchmarks for AI, in addition to the usual text-based measures. Both AI and robots also mix to provide ultra-realistic robots like AI-DA the robot painter [8, 9].

These examples demonstrate how addressing the arts can be challenging for AI researchers, particularly when a robot is involved. It is challenging because arts summon emotions and reach the deepest and most intimate part of our humanity. In some ways, visual and performing arts can be challenging for humans to interpret, so we need to tread carefully when introducing algorithms and AI into this domain. But it seems as if the arts offer a particularly rich opportunity for understanding the possibility of artificial sentience. The aim of our ongoing project is to try and outline a test to evaluate the sentient intelligence of robots.

Our goal here is not to conclusively describe a detailed test, but instead to suggest a method of investigation that has not been robustly considered yet. For example, in a broad-reaching survey of tests of machine consciousness, Elemrani and Yampoulskiy [10] taxonomize such tests under a number of qualities they might possess. Importantly, while creativity appears relevant to a (small) number of tests [11] the most famous of these tests focused on jazz improvisation. The phenomenological experience of social interaction in such tests is largely absent. Granted, there are some functional correlates that appear occasionally in such tests, where looking at both the architecture of the system and its subsequent behaviour can stand in for an evaluation of an experiencing subject, but such correlates are themselves uncommon and poorly discussed within such

---

[1] BladeRunner is a movie related to the universe from the novel "Do Androids Dream of Electric Sheep?" from Philip K. Dick (1968).

literature. This is probably true for at least two reasons: first, we have yet to create a test even for humans and animals such that we could conclusively claim to have solved the problem of other minds, and therefore creating such a test for machines is clearly out of reach until the problem is clarified or redefined. Second, because the literature in phenomenology tends to begin at the felt, conscious experience of the experiencer, it might appear to be an odd starting point for such a test. While we cannot claim to have solved these problems at all, we believe there is something about the participation (by dancer and spectator) in certain kinds of performance that indicate underlying conscious experience, and that some version of this can be mapped on to the quest for machine sentience. Our motivation, then, is to bring together three perspectives not generally seen together (computer science, choreography, and phenomenology) and to suggest a methodology in practice that can be applied to tests of machine sentience. We recognize much is going unsaid here, including detailed descriptions of what prerequisites must be present to even participate in such a test, including something like humanoid embodiment and dynamic systems to interact with the unpredictable world in real time. We instead start here from a provocation that the work in machine sentience or consciousness has not looked to performance studies or choreography yet in ways that might reveal new and unique ways of approaching the problem.

## 3   Choreography Analysis

We have tried to carefully study how the "Chemins à coulisses," a dance choreographed by Micheline Lelièvre, is played, more accurately implemented, and how parts of it work. The choreography is written for four performers. Each of them knows the overall partition. This dance is a quartet, performed in a square space. There is no music, except the sound of dancers' steps or their breathing. The video of the full performance can be seen at [12]. An explanation of the performance is provided on the following video [26].

Writing choreography means defining the steps to be executed, in which space and with which inner music. "Chemins à coulisses" is written using protocols like canon, repetition, and various changes of directions in space. This is quite common and easy to reproduce as required.

Each step of this dance is written, which means that the four dancers know exactly what they have to do. The choreography is built with different sequences and patterns, in which the performers slide and move in the choreographed space, but they also differ in the number of steps according to each dancer. They may dance all together the same steps at the same time, at the same pace, in different directions, or dance the same steps by pairs (in different spaces as well). But the core of the choreography remains elsewhere, and it is the most difficult part to explain, which plays into the ways this offers a mode of testing for sentience. Talking about the dance is extremely challenging, and, like explaining the blue color to someone who was born without vision, we hope to point toward non-propositional knowledge as a source of valuable insight into human sentience.

In this choreography, certain items are not specified, like speed of execution. This means that the dancers have to rely on different skills, and not only on memory. Dancers know when and where the movement begins. They have to finish the sequence together, but they can't always see their partners, sometimes in the dance, they turn their back. How do they accomplish that? The ability to do this is the result of long practice and training. But there are also a certain number of parameters or skills that dancers use to achieve it.

In the performance, the dancers are hearing each other, but this is neither necessary nor sufficient for a successful performance of the dance. Mostly, they use a kinesthetic sense to feel how their partners behave. The dancers are all related to the others through feelings, including breathing, sound of movements, and perception of air moving around. And finally, the dancers finish the sequence in time and together. The whole dance has its own musicality, which means inner rhythm, inner music inside the movement itself. The dance is made of all these parameters together. Any attempt to analyze and make sense of the dance and the experience of the dance requires that the viewer differentiate imitation from interpretation.

If the dancers were only to imitate movements and just have to know in which space, at what time to perform them, and at which pace, it would not match with the design of Micheline's choreography. Something more subtle is required here. Dancers have to coordinate together without speaking, and without seeing each other sometimes. Their ability to interpret the choreography is very important. The heart of the creation is the choreography itself and not the performer individually. The four dancers create something that can only happen through the way they are related, each one to the others, beyond any personal desire.

This is the point where we are not sure that robots can be able to be as creative as dancers are! For sure they can imitate the choreography; it is not difficult. But would robots be able to act and make decisions allowing the dance to generate something unexpected that brings emotion for the audience and to the dancers as well? There are larger questions here related to autonomy that, we think, must be answered. But the possibility that a robot is being able to interact, as a person does in this dance, would indicate that, if some semblances of autonomy were already present, then perhaps the robot is engaging in the dance in a genuine way. As a counterexample, see any of the videos that Boston Dynamics has released of their robots dancing together. You can see the impressive range of movement each robot is capable of, but you can also see that there is nothing but pre-programmed imitation, without dynamic interaction and the ability to feel changes in the co-participants in the dance. Eric Whitman, one of the roboticists involved in teaching the Boston Dynamics robots to dance together, said, [13] "Everything had to be worked out in advance and scripted precisely. Robots have the advantage over humans in that they're very repeatable: Once you get it right, it stays right. But they have the disadvantage that you have to tell them every little detail. They don't improvise at all."

## 4 Levels of Description

### 4.1 Choreography (Speaking as M. Lelièvre, Choreographer)

To choreograph is to create a situation that offers the possibility of a meeting. What is born from the encounter could not exist otherwise. This is what happens "between" the beings, the dancers, the public, and the places. What I would expect from a robot who would dance with us, would be that this object, (designed by humans) brings me (as the dancer) to a place of unexpected reflection and creation, by its specificity, as a different performer and in two-way exchange. So that it questions me-as-dancer, and simultaneously the encounter also modifies the robot.

It is undoubtedly a philosophical question and which questions what it means to be human living with other living beings and sharing an event with other living beings. To choreograph means to create a situation that offers the possibility of a meeting.

**Objects and Subjects.** The form of the robot is not important. I like to choreograph and perform with objects.

Once I helped a friend to create a dance with a cabbage. The cabbage in this case becomes a partner. It has its own way of being alive! It can be heavy, round or irregular in its form, fragile or not. All these parameters determine how one dances with this partner and how the choreographer constructs the dance according to the specificity of the two partners. Dancing with an object is to incorporate it, like a part of the moving body, an extension, or it can also create a space of interaction between the object and the dancer.

So, to dance with a robot, any form it would have would mean to know exactly what it is able to do and to construct the choreography according to these parameters. But to dance with a robot would not be like to dance with a human being. It is different because something is missing. And this missing something is what we're hoping can be captured and harnessed as a way to look for the presence of that missing something.

### 4.2 Social Cognition and Phenomenology (Speaking as R. Zebrowski, Cognitive Scientist and Philosopher)

Traditionally, much work in social cognition has focused on the internal lives of the interactors, treating social cognition as traditional cognition facing outward. However, the theory of participatory sense-making, a theory with roots in enactivism, offers a richer story of social dynamics. This view focuses, instead of on the minds of individuals in a social situation, on the autonomous social system that arises from (and as) that social situation [14]. Rather than trying to make sense of social experiences just through the intentions of the individuals, participatory sense-making focuses on the myriad ways the interaction itself takes over, sometimes working against the interactors and their intentions. The classic example here is when two people walk down a hallway toward one another, and in attempting to move out of the way, both instead mirror the moves of the other, frustrating the intentions of everyone involved.

These kinds of dynamic systems can be measured and modeled, and there's a way in which the choreography that Micheline describes here can work in a very similar way. She describes the dancers and the spectators as engaged in an embodied, affective reaction rather than a cognitive one; we already know people lack the kind of privileged access to our own minds that has long been theorized, but thinking about choreographed dancers as part of a larger dynamic system offers a new way to consider machine sentience. What's more, we can measure and observe these systems from the top-down, through the autonomous dynamic system that arises in the interaction of the dance, and also from bottom-up, through what [15] have called mutual incorporation: the phenomenological level of description of the very same dynamic system.

### 4.3 Distributed Systems (Speaking as E. Gressier Soudan, Computer Scientist)

Analysing the choreography Micheline designed and instantiated with performers sounds like watching the execution of a living distributed system, an unexpected kind of distributed system, but kind of. To start such an analysis, we need to provide a list of first criteria: control, coordination, order, determinism, and indeterminism also [16].

The design of the choreography first tells us that there is a set of behaviours expected from performers. The patterns that define the overall choreography invite the viewer to think that it is a deterministic execution. But, as the control belongs to each of the performers anytime, the result is not the same at each occurrence of the performance. Then, there is no total order [17] that drives the execution. Strictly speaking, the distributed execution can't be imitated and reproduced exactly the same each time.

Performers build their own synchronization all together, which is real time but not clock driven. They use an inner tempo, and their inner tempo self-synchronizes among the inner tempo of others. Self-Stabilizing algorithms are part of the distributed system domain [18]. The overall performance is self driven by messages the performers are exchanging breath, look around, noise from the movement of each other. What this means is that the execution self-stabilizes in the same way an autonomous system does. In a first approach, it is more a message-passing and event-driven distributed system. Except the knowledge of the full choreography before start, during performance no state information is explicitly or partially shared among dancers involving any information consistency management protocol [19].

Shared knowledge based distributed systems are emerging through the networked cyber physical systems paradigm [20]: enhanced crop growth control using robots and drones is an example of such an application. Do performers exchange knowledge when they execute the choreography? We can say yes. They build their own living map of the shared performance through the signals and events that their partners provide. It is not only signals and events, it is also the feeling of how the performance evolves, how their partners move to decide how they need to perform to be collectively right on the choreography purpose.

New research tries to enhance the responsiveness of Information and Communication Architectures. To deal with this goal, there have been attempts to model the evolving requirements of applications. Communication Networks evolves to be intent based [21] leading to intent mining using machine learning or federated machine learning techniques. Could we model the choreography using intention? Can we say that the choreography is an intent-based performance? A distributed system point of view is not enough to examine this last aspect. We need to address the performance with higher level tools that allow a better abstraction to take care of the inner semantic of performers' dance.

## 5  Analysis and Test of Machine Sentience

When Micheline describes the difference between dancing with objects and dancing with subjects, it's an illustration of what Fuchs and De Jaegher [15] terms mutual incorporation, which they define as, "a process in which the living bodies of both participants extend and form a common intercorporeality. [This kind of] intersubjectivity… is not a solitary task of deciphering of simulating the movements of others but means entering a process of embodied interaction and generating common meaning through it" [p. 465]. This is where we see these various levels of description overlapping to begin to offer us a way to approach a kind of test for machine sentience.

If we think about Micheline's description of the choreographed dance "chemins à coulisses", it is easy to see how this kind of interaction is not one of multiple mental states coming together to coordinate an interaction, but instead is a kind of embodied coordination that requires more than mere imitation. The performers in the dance know their movements, but must mesh with the others in the dance, giving up some of their autonomy for the sake of the larger system, in which each person embodies some part of the bodies of the others, and vice versa. As [15] put it, "In contrast to interactions with objects, which are only reactive- that is, they can change me but never because they intend to- in social interactions there is a certain way in which I am not in control... The other, while perceiving me and engaging with me, co-determines me in his gaze, touch, attitude, etc. I not only have limited control over the other, but also over myself in my encounter with him" [p. 477]. Think here of the difference between dancing with a cabbage (or an early 21st century robot) and dancing with another (or several other) human dancers. In the case of objects, there can be a kind of unidirectional incorporation, where I take up the body of the robot (or the cabbage) in my own embodied engagement with the world; but in the case of these reactive systems, there is no two-way intercorporeality. With another living body, we can understand the kinds of give and take required to perform such a dance, and the affective and embodied response that lets go of some amount of control for the sake of the interaction in general. We allow others in the choreography (and even among the spectators) to shape part of the dance, and in doing so we both recognize the subjectivity of the others, and also allow ourselves to be partially (and quite literally) determined by them in those moments. Will sentient robots be able to enter such behavior, and also this internal state perhaps?

## 6  Conclusion

We spoke earlier about how there are almost no tests of machine sentience that start at the creative or performative level. But there have been a number of robots used to stand in for human performers in plays, for example [22, 23, 24]. Yet by nearly universal account, those robots fail to do more than a set of mechanical pre-programmed responses, with no creativity or improvisation, and, more importantly, with no sense of genuine intersubjectivity or mutual incorporation. Thus far, robots have merely imitated, and not interpreted, these performances. No test of machine sentience is going to indicate anything interesting is happening in those performances. However, a dance, like the one we've been discussing here, offers an interesting moment for the emergence of genuine intersubjectivity.

The transversality of all this research opens the creativity and the subtlety of creation and interpretation. It makes concrete that art is a different way of thinking and the conversation between science, philosophy and choreography can be very inspiring.

Putting a robot in place of one of the dancers will offer a chance to see how dynamic the system is, but also to see how well attuned it is to the affect and embodiment of the dance partner. These are fine-tuned, sub-linguistic ways of interacting, and even people are not always successful at interpreting them. To that end, it probably matters more that a machine might pass this sort of test, and it means relatively little if it fails.

# References

1. Rushby, J., Sanchez, D.: Technology and Consciousness, SRI-CSL Technical Report (2018)
2. Feinberg, T.E.J.M., Mallatt, J.M.: The Ancient Origins of Consciousness: How the Brain Created Experience, MIT Press, Cambridge, p. 392 (2016)
3. Turing, A.: Computing Machinery and Intelligence. Oxford University Press, Mind, vol. 59, n. 236 (1950). https://doi.org/10.1093/mind/LIX.236.433
4. EuroScience Open Forum, ESOF2020 Trieste, 2–6 September 2020, Creative Explorations in Artificial Intelligence, Robotics, and Autonomous Systems Saturday, THEME I: COMPUTE THEREFORE I AM. September 5 - 18:00–19:30. Virtual Room 3. Coordinator John Murray, University of San José. USA (2020)
5. Gal, V.: Vers une nouvelle Interaction Humain Environnement dans les jeux vidéo et pervasifs: rétroaction biologique et états émotionnels. Defended December 9th 2019. CNAM. Paris. France (in french)
6. RoboCup: Objective. https://www.robocup.org/objective. Accessed 12 Apr 2022
7. Weinbach, A.: Computer Network class, teaching unit RSX102. Cloud Services : the Microsoft Azure offer. The Vincent Gan Gogh experience. May 31st (2019). CNAM Paris. https://www.instagram.com/vincentgangogh/?hl=fr. Accessed 12 Apr 2022
8. Haynes, S.: This robot artist just became the first to stage a solo exhibition (2019). https://time.com/5607191/robot-artist-ai-da-artificial-intelligence-creativity/. Accessed 15 Apr 2022
9. Meet Ai-Da. ai-darobot.com. Accessed 15 Apr 2022
10. Elemrani, A., Yampolskiy, R.: Reviewing tests for machine consciousness (2018). https://www.researchgate.net/publication/325498266_Reviewing_Tests_for_Machine_Consciousness. Accessed 15 Apr 2022
11. Chella, A., Manzotti, R.: AGI and machine consciousness. Theor. Found. Artif. Gen. Intell. 4, 263–282 (2012)
12. Lelièvre, M.: Chemins à coulisses (2020). https://vimeo.com/339317571.9mn36. Accessed 12 Apr 2022
13. Hennick, C.: All together now (2021). https://blog.bostondynamics.com/all-together-now. Accessed 15 Apr 2022
14. De Jaegher, H., Di Paolo, E.: Participatory sense-making: an enactive approach to social cognition. Phenomenol. Cogn. Sci. 6(4), 485–507 (2007). https://doi.org/10.1007/s11097-007-9076-9
15. Fuchs, T., De Jaegher, H.: Enactive intersubjectivity: participatory sense-making and mutual incorporation. Phenomenol. Cogn. Sci. 8, 465–486 (2009)
16. Raynal, M.: Distributed Algorithms for Message-Passing Systems. Springer, Berlin (2013). https://doi.org/10.1007/978-3-642-38123-2
17. Lamport, L.: Time, clocks, and the ordering of events in a distributed system. In: Communications of the ACM, V21N7, July 1978
18. Tixeuil, S.: Algorithms and Theory of Computation Handbook, Second Edition, chapter Self-stabilizing Algorithms, pp. 26.1–26.45. Chapman & Hall/CRC Applied Algorithms and Data Structures. CRC Press, Taylor & Francis Group, November (2009)
19. Aldin, H.N.S., Deldari, H., Moattar, M.H., Ghods, M.R.: Consistency models in distributed systems: a survey on definitions, disciplines, challenges and applications, 12 February 2019. https://arxiv.org/pdf/1902.03305.pdf

20. Stehr, M.-O., Kim, M., Talcott, C.: Partially ordered knowledge sharing and fractionated systems in the context of other models for distributed computing. In: Iida, S., Meseguer, J., Ogata, K. (eds.) Specification, Algebra, and Software. LNCS, vol. 8373, pp. 402–433. Springer, Heidelberg (2014). https://doi.org/10.1007/978-3-642-54624-2_20
21. Pang, L., Yang, C., Chen, D., Song, Y., Guizani, M.: A survey on intent-driven networks. IEEE. https://ieeexplore.ieee.org/stamp/stamp.jsp?arnumber=8968429. Accessed 12 Apr 2022
22. Petrović, D., Kićinbaći, L., Petric, F., Kovačić, Z.: Autonomous robots as actors in robotics theatre - tribute to the centenary of R.U.R. In: 2019 European Conference on Mobile Robots (ECMR), Prague, Czech Republic, 2019, pp. 1–7 (2019). https://doi.org/10.1109/ECMR.2019.8870908
23. Spedalieri, F.: Quietly posthuman: oriza hirata's robot-theatre. Perform. Res. **19**(2), 138–140 (2014). https://doi.org/10.1080/13528165.2014.928530
24. Japan Society: Double bill of one-act plays features android, robot, and human actors (2013). https://www.japansociety.org/page/about/press/double-bill-of-one-acts. Accessed 30 Nov 2020
25. Kornyshova, E., Gressier, S.E.: Introducing sentient requirements for information systems and digital technologies. EMCIS **2021**, 384–395 (2021)
26. Lelièvre, M.: Chemins à Coulisses with two performers, described by Micheline Lelièvre (2020). https://vimeo.com/484858770/f374120c2a.2mn. Accessed 12 Apr 2022

KET4DF 2022

# The 4th International Workshop on Key Enabling Technologies for Digital Factories (KET4DF 2022)

## Preface

The manufacturing industry is entering a new digital era in which advanced information systems and especially (big) data-driven methods and artificial intelligence (AI) techniques allow companies to move beyond distributed and supervisory control systems to support significant operational improvements and allow dynamic adaptability.

This translates not only into a strong technological evolution but also into an unprecedented extension of companies' information systems. Exploitation of data and services derived from disparate and distributed sources, development of scalable and efficient real-time systems, management of expert knowledge, advanced data analytics, and optimized decision making are some of the key challenges which advanced information systems can address in an effort to reach the vision of a digital revolution in manufacturing.

Moreover, human-centered trustworthy AI systems provide the ability to augment human work and extend human capabilities in order to solve problems and achieve goals that were unreachable by either humans or machines alone. Such efforts may allow the manufacturing industry in the post-COVID era to "go back to normal" and optimize, scale, and adapt their processes and services towards a circular and resilient economy.

The goal of this workshop is to attract high-quality research papers focusing on advanced information systems for digital factories and smart manufacturing. The idea of the workshop was born to promote the research topics of some international projects, which have also become the supporters of the workshop: FIRST (H2020 grant # 734599), COALA (H2020 grant #957296), STAR (H2020 grant #956573), and XMANAI (H2020 grant #957362).

The KET4DF 2022 proceedings include three papers addressing different topics related to digital factories. The first shows how digital twins can enhance the resilience and improve the overall security posture of the manufacturing industry, in the very critical domain of aerospace. The second paper addresses zero defect manufacturing, a manufacturing process to continuously improve the product design in order to increase quality guarantees. The third paper presents the exploitation of digital twins to achieve sustainable industry in different domains such as manufacturing, healthcare, and construction.

We are grateful to the CAiSE 2022 Workshop Chairs, Jelena Zdravkovic, Jennifer Horkoff, and Estefania Serral, for their precious support and to the members of the Program Committee for their contribution.

June 2022

Giacomo Cabri
Karl Hribernik
Federica Mandreoli
Gregoris Mentzas

# Organization

## Workshop Organizers

Federica Mandreoli             Università di Modena e Reggio Emilia, Italy
Giacomo Cabri                Università di Modena e Reggio Emilia, Italy
Gregoris Mentzas           National Technical University of Athens,
                                   Greece
Karl Hribernik                Bremer Institut für Produktion und Logistik
                                   GmbH, Germany

## Program Committee

Marco Aiello                 University of Stuttgart, Germany
Kosmas Alexopoulos       University of Patras, Greece
Dimitris Apostolou         University of Piraeus, Greece
Yuewei Bai                  Shanghai Polytechnic University, China
Alexandros Bousdekis      National Technical University of Athens,
                                   Greece
Fenareti Lampathaki        Suite5, Cyprus
Hervé Panetto              University of Lorraine
Pierluigi Plebani           Politechnico di Milano, Italy
Ioannis Soldatos            Intrasoft International
Walter Terkaj               STIIMA-CNR, Italy
Lai Xu                        Bournemouth University, UK
Stefan Wellsandt           Bremer Institut für Produktion und Logistik
                                   GmbH, Germany

# Digital Twins for Enhanced Resilience: Aerospace Manufacturing Scenario

Adrien Bécue[1], Martin Praddaude[1], Eva Maia[2(✉)], Nicolas Hogrel[1], Isabel Praça[2], and Reda Yaich[3]

[1] Airbus Cybersecurity SAS, Elancourt, France
[2] GECAD/ISEP, Porto, Portugal
egm@isep.ipp.pt
[3] IRT SystemX, Rennes, France

**Abstract.** European manufacturing industry faces a growing cyber-threat landscape which increasingly involves sophisticated nation-state-sponsored actors. Moreover, while the ongoing evolution towards more connected production environments generates significant benefits in productivity, it also creates more complex risk scenarios. In this work we show how Digital Twins enhance the resilience and improve the overall security posture of manufacturing industry, based on a highly critical scenario unfolding in the aerospace sector.

**Keywords:** Digital Twin · Distributed manufacturing · Cyber resilience

## 1 Introduction

The 4th industrial revolution is characterized by enhanced connectivity and autonomy of production systems [7]. In this context, the adoption of Industrial Internet of things (IIoT) [8] contributes to bridging the gap between enterprise Information Technology (IT) and Operational Technology (OT) [17]. An undesired effect of this is the widening of the attack surface of industrial systems [29]. SeCoIIA Project [1] aims at solving this dilemma by securing digital transition of manufacturing industry towards more connected, collaborative, flexible and automated production techniques. The restrictions applying to equipment in operations form a major obstacle to secure connectivity deployment in manufacturing OT. In particular, active security testing is most commonly prohibited and manufacturing data are kept confidential. An interesting solution proposed by the literature is the involvement of Digital Twins (DT) in support to OT security operations [5,6]. Yet to the best of our knowledge, there has been no

This project has received funding from the European Union's Horizon 2020 research and innovation programme under grant agreement No. 871967. This output reflects the views only of the author(s), and the European Union cannot be held responsible for any use which may be made of the information contained therein. For more information on the project see: https://secoiia.eu/.

J. Horkoff et al. (Eds.): CAiSE 2022, LNBIP 451, pp. 107–118, 2022.
https://doi.org/10.1007/978-3-031-07478-3_9

successful implementation of DTs for security assurance of manufacturing OT at this stage. With this work, we aim to demonstrate the feasibility and value added of simulation-based security assurance for legacy OT integration into an Industrial IoT system, using DTs and CRs. It will contribute to research by providing techniques for modelling highly heterogeneous OT environments and conducting realistic attack scenarios. It will contribute to practice, by enabling simulation-based security decision support for OT professionals involved in digital transformation programs. An important benefit for the industry will be the ability for complex supply chains to adopt collaborative manufacturing techniques without compromising their physical assets and confidential data Fig. 1). DTs of both the manufacturing equipment and the end product can be leveraged to perform security assurance in a collaborative manner throughout the lifecycle of complex systems, erasing the blind spots of current security practice.

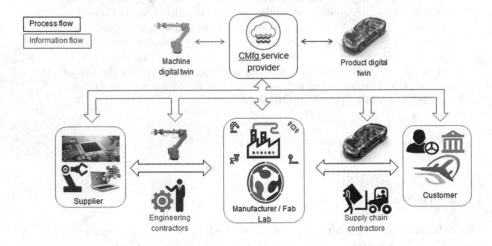

**Fig. 1.** SeCoIIA Collaborative Manufacturing ecosystem

To ensure the operational relevance and applicability of the innovations, the SeCoIIA project developments were driven by practical use-cases from 3 industries: Aerospace, Automotive and Maritime systems manufacturing. In this paper we make a focus on the application to the aerospace manufacturing use-case which deals with IIoT deployment in Airbus Defence and Space factories of Tablada, San Pablo Sur, and Cadiz. With this example, we demonstrate that DT effectively support industries to improve their cybersecurity, in parallel to the deployment of connected and collaborative manufacturing techniques.

The remaining paper is structured as follows: Section 2 gives an overview of the industrial use-cases addressed. Section 3 provides the state of the art in matters of OT with a focus on simulation and collaboration. Section 4 provides evidence of successful implementation of DTs in support to security decision. The conclusion provides a summary of the findings, evidence of progress beyond the state of the art and areas for future research.

## 2   Aerospace Scenario Description

The Aerospace domain needs to deal with the deployment of several IIoT components ensuring the correct functioning of collaborative robotics. Therefore, it is mandatory to improve productivity safety and security and to manage collaborative robots to support human operators in logistic, drilling and riveting activities. In this section we define an aerospace scenario, describing the sequence of actions usual taken by normal users in the manufacturing environment. Then, we extend this use case with a misuse case to effective address the security requirements, focusing on the exceptions and threats that can be caused by hostile agents.

### 2.1   Use-case

Airbus Defence and Space owns several sites in Spain which are dedicated to the production and the final assembly of commercial and military aircraft. Airbus Defence and Space factories of Tablada, San Pablo Sur, and Cadiz have launched an important digital transformation program which relies on the deployment of a multi-site and multi-asset IIoT platform to support enhanced automation, optimization, and quality control on sensitive industrial processes involved in the manufacturing of flight-safety critical aeronautical parts. This multi-asset IIoT platform is composed of three industrial assets known as: Roboshave, Autoclave, and Gap Gun (see Fig. 2). For the purpose of this paper, we will focus on the IIoT implementation to the Roboshave system (upper left in Fig. 2). The Roboshave system has been implemented in the Tablada plant to automate rivet shaving operations on rudders. Rivet shaving is an impractical and time consuming operations which slows down the complete production line if performed manually [28]. The rivets have to be as flat as possible and to remain within tolerances specified in the requirements [30]. For that, each rivet is manually shaved to give the rudder the essential aerodynamic characteristics required by for such an aircraft part.

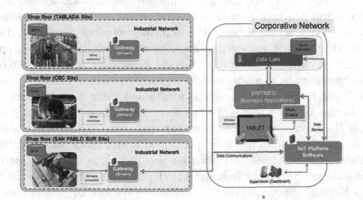

**Fig. 2.** Airbus defence and space IIoT system overview

The objective of this use case is to improve the automation between the Roboshave and corporate system and to secure the communication and data in different systems. The automation of this process by means of a robotic system connected to an IIoT platform helps fulfilling the following objectives: 1) enable remote production monitoring and control, 2) optimize the industrial process based on historical data, 3) automate maintenance reporting, 4) demonstrate simulation-based security enforcement.

## 2.2  Misuse-case

As introduced earlier, the digitization program is expected to bear consequences on industrial systems security. During SeCoIIA project execution, a risk analysis was conducted in order to identify existing and future possible misuse-cases that should be considered for security enhancement. It was fulfilled according to IEC62443 [12] standards which aim to secure industrial automation and control systems (IACS) throughout their lifecycle. It starts by drawing assumptions about the nominal use-case implementation, then describes the attacker in terms of skills, means and motivations, derives the attacker Tools and Techniques and Procedures (TTPs), describes the impact on business flow and provides suggestions for mitigation actions. For the purpose of this paper, we focus here on the misuse of the Roboshave system described above.

**Assumptions** the industrial system is highly predictable, uses a limited number of protocols, very well-known and stable over time. The network is secured by WPA2 and can be broken with a dictionary attack. The industrial means connected to the IIoT platform are already configured as part of the network and the used protocols and frameworks are configured as standard with no individual extensions or adaptions. Authentication of the industrial means is not considered. If authentication is used, it should be the same for all of them. The wireless communication between the industrial means and the IIoT platform is vulnerable and acts as an entrance gate into the further backend.

**Attacker** The observed attacker in this misuse case has knowledge about the communication protocol as well as the industrial environment. Furthermore, he has knowledge about networks (specifically wireless networks). He wants to disrupt the production environment, prove his skills as well as spoof the IIoT Communication. The attacker has the knowledge to develop an offensive machine learning algorithm which will stay as a persistent threat on the Industrial IIoT platform. Considering the mentioned skills and in relation to the IEC62443 the attacker is classified as level 3 attacker. The Level 3 attacker, known as Hacktivist, drives intentional attacks, with sophisticated means and moderate resources, and has ICS specific skills and moderate motivation.

**TTPs** The analysis focuses on risks that are linked to the introduction of a misconfiguration file on the Industrial IIoT platform software, on the PC that contains Kepware Server, or on the Roboshave system, by insider threat, Man in the Middle (MitM) attack and/or adversarial machine learning. Relying on smart sensing and IIoT for safety-critical manufacturing processes would potentially increase exposure to attacks exploiting the lack of authentication security of state of the art sensor networks. A skilled attacker could insert a rogue device to gain access to the IIoT network and spy the production network to gain privileges.

**Impact** The attacker could spy, interrupt, jam or spoof the IIoT communication, leading to production downtime, quality of even safety problems.

## 3 Digital Twins in Industry

Back to the 'mirrored systems' developed by NASA for the ill-fated 1970 Apollo 13 space project [3], the digital twin has come a reality applied to different domains in the last decade. DT are based on the usage of several different technologies, such as machine learning and simulation, able to support a digital replica of a systems and benefiting from a real-time integration with the physical components. Industrial applications of DT focus on areas such as predictive maintenance, process optimization and safety manegement [9,19], also with specific applications in the aviation sector. As replicas of the real systems, DT provide an environment suitable also to test the cybersecurity and resilience of systems. For example, Eckhart et al. [15] used DT paradigm as a tool for situational awareness, and Xu et al. [33] proposed ATTAIN, a DT to analyze live data and detect anomalies. Our initial approach [22] is different, as it focus on a DT based on CyberRange (CR) technology applied to a specific use case in the aerospace industry. Next section introduces our concept.

### 3.1 CyberRange Based Digital Twin for Simulation-Based Security Decision

Abundant literature covers the use of cyber-security simulation systems commonly called Cyber Ranges (CR). The concept of CR takes its roots in an analogy with Shooting Ranges, which are specialized facilities designed for firearms qualifications, training or practice [31]. Hence, CRs have primarily been used for cyber-security training [25]. However, an IT network simulation capacity realistic enough to support training of cyber-security professionals, can equally serve a number of other use-cases. CRs have been used extensively in cyber-security research [20], as testbeds for the demonstration of new security products [16], as testing environment for the certification of IT and security equipment [32], and as instruments for decision making in incident response [18]. The classical attributes of a CR are: i) a computing platform which can be stationary, mobile, or cloud-based; ii) a traffic generator which injects real or emulated traffic, iii) Virtual Machines (VMs) which support virtual network population with realistic assets; iv) catalogues of templates for hardware, firmware, software, and threats modelling; and v) a design interface enabling intuitive topology construction; a physical switch or interface enabling to plug physical assets which can be embedded in hybrid simulation scenarios [6]. Some examples of CRs are Hynesim from Diateam, Malice from Sysdream, Palo Alto Cyber Range, Ravello Cyber Range,

Cisco Cyber Range, Cdex Cyber Range by Vector Synergy. Despite all the benefits, several limitations of next-generation CRs are known, such as the lack of open standard and interoperability, the complexity of deployment, lack of collaborative scenario modelling capacity, and the lack of realistic modelling of OT environments [6].

Nonetheless, it has been forecasted that OT environments could be effectively addressed by the combination of CRs and DT [5]. According to Rovere et al. [27] the DT is the semantic, functional, and simulation-ready representation of shop floor Cyber-Physical Systems (CPS). According to Malakuti et al., the DT can be used throughout the manufacturing life cycle for design, production, operation, and maintenance purposes [22]. Some noticeable DT solutions are proposed by General Electric, PTC Windchill, Dassault Systemes 3DS, Microsoft Azure, Ansys Software, IBM Digital Twin Exchange, Factory I/O, and Siemens.

The prevalence of proprietary solutions commercialized by automation and computing vendors constitutes one of the remaining limiting factors to DT adoption by the industry. Indeed, proper implementation of the DT concept would require open source technology or at least established standards for interoperability. A few initiatives towards open source DT technology should be mentioned. Damjanovic-Behrendt and Behrendt [13] proposed an open source DT concept base on a micro-services architecture. Another reference architecture was introduced by the consortium of the research project MAYA [27] with actable functional and behavioral CPS models. Also the research project AUTOWARE [23] developed a cognitive digital automation operation system embedded networked DT. As already mentioned, the possible use of DTs in combination with CRs for security operation purposes has been suggested by several studies [5,6], since this combination could support the modelling of effects of a cyber incident affecting complex manufacturing systems throughout their physical and logical dimensions [14]. However, we are not aware of any convincing demonstration of simulation-based security decision support with application to OT security operations to date.

In the development of a digital twin, the notion of fidelity level is essential. Indeed, twins cannot be judged in a Manichean way. Each will have significant differences that will result in advantages and disadvantages in their respective use. For example, a physical twin will have the advantage of being completely integrated with the original process, whereas the digital twin will have to adapt to strong constraints of compatibility and verisimilitude in relation to the medium on which it is based. On the other hand, the physical twin will often be unavailable, and above all, it is dangerous to apply tests for which the consequences are too uncertain. The digital twin can be completely manipulated at will, can be saved in different states to perform multiple tests, and tends to show the potential consequences according to the actions performed upstream. We can thus define different types of metrics such as technical, functional or business metrics, which will allow us to judge whether the digital twin built corresponds to the expectations of the project, with the expected level of quality in the simulation rendering that it proposes.

# 4  Digital Twin Application in Aerospace Manufacturing

As pointed out in the previous section, a significant body of previous work has demonstrated DTs in support of manufacturing operations, but without evidence of their practical use for OT security enforcement [6]. One of the goals of SeCoIIA project was to prove that DTs can effectively support security enforcement, notably at design, commissioning, and execution stages of an industrial digitization program. In this section we will provide a detailed description of the modelling and simulation work carried out to demonstrate this DTs capability.

## 4.1  Roboshave System Simulation

In this work, we used Airbus CR as a modelling simulation environment. The CR offers an extensive catalogue of virtual assets (virtual machines and containers) and virtual network appliances to simulate and emulate a wide variety of IT (Information Technology) and OT (Operational Technology) systems. The CR also encapsulates a catalogue of attacks and traffic emulators. Combining these capabilities offers a realistic and immersive digital twin experience that maximizes the impact of simulation and enhances the cybersecurity posture of digital manufacturing actors. The simulation work has been carried out in continuous interaction with Roboshave operators, enabling the verification of the validity and value of the DT at any time during construction by having it tested and adopted by manufacturing practitioners [4]. The list of physical assets present in the system which need to be included in the scope of simulation, includes a FANUC robotic arm, a Gocator profilometer, a safety SICK AG PLC, a Siemens PLC, and a Siemens HMI.

It was ensured that as much information as possible was gathered about the employed components: equipment manufacturer, product version, technical characteristics, operation modes, hardware and software, connectivity, etc. [26]. In addition, the endemic parts to Roboshave such as the PLC and HMI projects, but also the various descriptions on the functionalities of the process were recovered. The description of the operations that can subsequently be used in cyber security scenarios were obtained, such as the different nominal/degraded modes, the segregation of roles in the management of the process, or the expected behavior of the system [21]. Furthermore, information related to interactions between different assets was considered [2]. Once the industrial system has been understood in depth, the DT was built reproducing all elements of its Physical Twin (TW).

Apart from intrinsic component processes, system connectivity also required comprehensive simulation (Fig. 3). Important links that have been modelled are: i) the S7Comm link between PLCSimAdv (PLC) and WinCC (HMI) to exchange process data; ii) the S7Comm link between WinCC (HMI) and EWS to load Siemens project; iii) the S7Comm link between PLCSimAdv (PLC) and EWS to load Siemens project; iv) the Modbus TCP link between PLCSimAdv (PLC) and Airbus Cyber-Security simulator (Profilometer); v) the Profinet link between PLC and Robot/Safety PLC. All these elements contribute to an increase in the quality and fidelity levels of the model. Several protocols in use within this list were not supported by vendor solutions (see Fig. 4). This is how the development of our own Profinet simulation stack was launched. This work resulted in a system allowing to capture the communicating devices in Profinet on a network, and to establish a relation between the sub-systems. The Profinet layer developed by Airbus CyberSecurity supports certain functionalities resulting from the specifications indicated in IEC 61158-5-10 [10] and IEC 61158-6-10 [11]. These complex developments allow the model to propose an even larger number of possible scenarios applicable on the simulation.

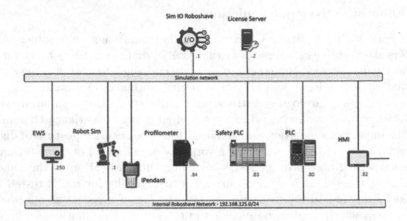

**Fig. 3.** Roboshave digital twin topology view

## 4.2   Roboshave System Resilience

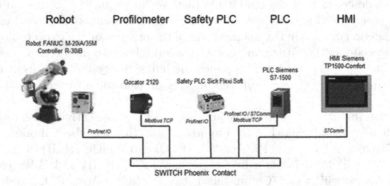

**Fig. 4.** Roboshave system connectivity overview

Using the misuse case previously described as guide, we have implemented different cyber-attacks. By taking into account the integration constraints related to the fidelity level, a scope for cyber-attacks could be defined as relevant or not. In the event that an attacker reaches the Roboshave internal network, the attacker would have the possibility of practicing common attacks in IT, but also functional in OT environments such as Man-In-The-Middle through ARP (Address Resolution Protocol) poisoning between components, in order to spy on exchanged business data [24], or cut off the corresponding communications, and thus put the industrial system to an unstable state. The possible consequences of this attack can be loss of the industrial process control, and/or impacting the safety. Based on an analysis, we have defined and implemented the following attack scenario in the simulation environment, separated by different single actions:

1. Removing the connectivity between PLC and HMI of Roboshave. It results on a loss of remote control by operators, and the monitoring values available in the PLC are not raised on the HMI anymore
2. From the attacker machine, writing on the HMI's industrial variables to display wrong information. These ones will be raised into the Corporative Network, and not overwrite by the PLC because of the last action (Fig. 5)

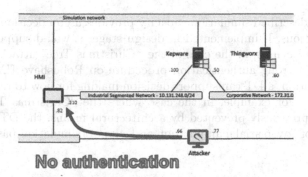

**Fig. 5.** Christmas tree attack implementation in the simulation environment

This attack is called "Christmas Tree" for the reason that it turns rivet status indicator lights multicolor like Christmas tree ornaments on the Roboshave user interface (see Fig. 6). The attack exploits an identified weakness in the implementation of an OT protocol, which lacks an authentication procedure on the Roboshave HMI. On the nominal system, each rudder shaving score is identified under a tablet. Before the shaving process, each tablet should be red (0%), and after, each tablet should be in blue (100%). These tablets are stored in the server of the HMI with an array of integers. Because of the lack of authentication, it is possible to access and read these data, and write on them a new value. The common default configuration in OT protocols are no authentication and no encryption. So some functions are available and ready to use, like read and write on tags, and so tablets on the HMI. For demonstration purpose, the manipulation of shaving data is here made very visible (Fig. 6). However, an attacker meaning to harm would likely modify statistics in a stealthier manner, so that the attack goes undetected. It would cause shaving defaults to run undetected and/or successful shaving operations to be reported faulty, leading in one case to non-conformance and flight safety risks, in the other case to rework and confusion in the manufacturing process.

**Fig. 6.** Roboshave interface nominal shaving condition & Christmas tree attack

The above described simulation capacity provides useful decision support for security operations. If implemented in design stage, it would support architectural decisions, such as, in the case of the "Christmas Tree" attack, the implementation of a strong authentication procedure on Roboshave HMI. If maintained in operation, a DT can support decision making for how to react to unexpected attacks. For example, in the case where the "Christmas Tree" attack had not been previously prevented by architectural means, the DT would provide evidence of adversarial manipulation and support simulation-based response selection.

## 5    Conclusion

This paper provides evidence of progress beyond the state of the art of using DTs in the manufacturing environment, enhancing resilience and improving the overall security posture of the manufacturing industry. An important contribution of this work is the demonstration of realistic attacks in simulation environment which helped designing security measures and countermeasures without affecting industrial operations. The described use case is just a sample of a broad scope of demonstrations that encompass four sectoral pilot use cases executed within the scope of the SeCoIIA project on aerospace, automotive, naval and robotics manufacturing systems. The industrial assets and protocols addressed are relatively widespread which ensures reusability and applicability of the results in a wide range of in- dustrial use cases. The fact that these implementations have been made in close interaction with Airbus manufacturing professionals is a guarantee of accuracy and applicability of the results. A remaining limitation is that the current DT is not connected to the physical system in real time. This limitation prevents DT application for continuous monitoring of OT system security. Further research shall be carried to involve the DT in real time monitoring and response enforcement within a collaborative OT Security Operation Center (SOC) infrastructure. For this purpose, defensive measures need to be taken against attacks that would target the communication link between the physical assets and the simulation environment.

# References

1. SeCoIIA: Secure collaborative intelligent industrial assets. https://secoiia.eu/
2. Bao, J., Guo, D., Li, J., Zhang, J.: The modelling and operations for the digital twin in the context of manufacturing. Enterp. Inf. Syst. **13**(4), 534–556 (2019)
3. Barricelli, B.R., Casiraghi, E., Fogli, D.: A survey on digital twin: definitions, characteristics, applications, and design implications. IEEE Access **7**, 167653–167671 (2019)
4. Bärring, M., Johansson, B., Shao, G.: Digital twin for smart manufacturing: the practitioner's perspective. In: ASME International Mechanical Engineering Congress and Exposition, vol. 84492, p. V02BT02A015. American Society of Mechanical Engineers (2020)
5. Becue, A., et al.: Cyberfactory# 1-securing the industry 4.0 with cyber-ranges and digital twins. In: 2018 14th IEEE International Workshop on Factory Communication Systems (WFCS), pp. 1–4. IEEE (2018)
6. Becue, A., Maia, E., Feeken, L., Borchers, P., Praca, I.: A new concept of digital twin supporting optimization and resilience of factories of the future. Appl. Sci. **10**(13), 4482 (2020)
7. Bloem, J., Van Doorn, M., Duivestein, S., Excoffier, D., Maas, R., Van Ommeren, E.: The fourth industrial revolution: Things to tighten the link between it and OT. Sogeti VINT2014 (2014)
8. Boyes, H., Hallaq, B., Cunningham, J., Watson, T.: The industrial internet of things (IIOT): an analysis framework. Comput. Ind. **101**, 1–12 (2018)
9. Commission, E., Centre, J.R., Nativi, S., Craglia, M., Delipetrev, B.: Destination Earth : survey on "Digital Twins" technologies and activities, in the Green Deal area. Publications Office (2020)
10. Commission, I.E.: Iec 61158-5-10, July 2014
11. Commission, I.E.: Iec 61158-6-10, July 2019
12. Commission, I.E.: Iec 62443 (2021)
13. Damjanovic-Behrendt, V., Behrendt, W.: An open source approach to the design and implementation of digital twins for smart manufacturing. Int. J. Comput. Integr. Manuf. **32**(4–5), 366–384 (2019)
14. Eckhart, M., Ekelhart, A.: A specification-based state replication approach for digital twins. In: Proceedings of the 2018 Workshop on Cyber-Physical Systems Security and Privacy, pp. 36–47 (2018)
15. Eckhart, M., Ekelhart, A., Weippl, E.: Enhancing cyber situational awareness for cyber-physical systems through digital twins. In: 2019 24th ETFA (2019)

16. Hallaq, B., Nicholson, A., Smith, R., Maglaras, L., Janicke, H., Jones, K.: Cyran: a hybrid cyber range for testing security on ICS/SCADA systems. In: Cyber Security and Threats: Concepts, Methodologies, Tools, and Applications, pp. 622–637. IGI Global (2018)

17. Kamal, S., Al Mubarak, S., Scodova, B., Naik, P., Flichy, P., Coffin, G.: It and OT convergence-opportunities and challenges. In: SPE Intelligent Energy International Conference and Exhibition, OnePetro (2016)

18. Kavak, H., Padilla, J.J., Vernon-Bido, D., Gore, R., Diallo, S.: A characterization of cybersecurity simulation scenarios. In: SpringSim (CNS), p. 3 (2016)

19. Kritzinger, W., Karner, M., Traar, G., Henjes, J., Sihn, W.: Digital twin in manufacturing: a categorical literature review and classification. IFAC-PapersOnLine **51**(11), 1016–1022 (2018)

20. Leitner, M., et al.: Ait cyber range: flexible cyber security environment for exercises, training and research. In: Proceedings of the European Interdisciplinary Cybersecurity Conference, pp. 1–6 (2020)

21. Lou, X., Guo, Y., Gao, Y., Waedt, K., Parekh, M.: An idea of using digital twin to perform the functional safety and cybersecurity analysis. In: INFORMATIK 2019. Gesellschaft für Informatik eV (2019)

22. Malakuti, S., et al.: Digital twins for industrial applications. Definition Bus. Values Des. Aspects Stan. Use Cases. Version **1**, 1–19 (2020)

23. Molina, E., et al.: The AUTOWARE framework and requirements for the cognitive digital automation. In: Camarinha-Matos, L.M., Afsarmanesh, H., Fornasiero, R. (eds.) PRO-VE 2017. IAICT, vol. 506, pp. 107–117. Springer, Cham (2017). https://doi.org/10.1007/978-3-319-65151-4_10

24. Nam, S.Y., Jurayev, S., Kim, S.S., Choi, K., Choi, G.S.: Mitigating ARP poisoning-based man-in-the-middle attacks in wired or wireless LAN. EURASIP J. Wirel. Commun. Networking **2012**(1), 1–17 (2012)

25. Pham, C., Tang, D., Chinen, K.i., Beuran, R.: Cyris: A cyber range instantiation system for facilitating security training. In: SoICT, pp. 251–258 (2016)

26. Rodič, B.: Industry 4.0 and the new simulation modelling paradigm. Organizacija **50**(3), 193–207 (2017)

27. Rovere, D., Pedrazzoli, P., dal Maso, G., Alge, M., Ciavotta, M.: A centralized support infrastructure (CSI) to manage cps digital twin, towards the synchronization between cps deployed on the shopfloor and their digital representation. Digital Shopfloor Ind. Autom. Ind. **4**, 317–335 (2019)

28. Sarh, B., Buttrick, J., Munk, C., Bossi, R.: Aircraft manufacturing and assembly. In: Nof, S. (eds) Springer Handbook of Automation. Springer Handbooks, pp. 893–910. Springer, Berlin (2009). https://doi.org/10.1007/978-3-540-78831-7_51

29. Sisinni, E., Saifullah, A., Han, S., Jennehag, U., Gidlund, M.: Industrial internet of things: challenges, opportunities, and directions. IEEE Trans. Ind. Inf. **14**(11), 4724–4734 (2018)

30. Sterkenburg, R., Wang, P.H.: Standard Aircraft Handbook for Mechanics and Technicians. McGraw-Hill Education, New York (2021)

31. Tian, Z., et al.: A real-time correlation of host-level events in cyber range service for smart campus. IEEE Access **6**, 35355–35364 (2018)

32. Vykopal, J., Ošlejšek, R., Čeleda, P., Vizvary, M., Tovarňák, D.: Kypo cyber range: design and use cases (2017)

33. Xu, Q., Ali, S., Yue, T.: Digital twin-based anomaly detection in cyber-physical systems. In: 2021 14th IEEE ICST, pp. 205–216 (2021)

# Supporting Zero Defect Manufacturing Through Cloud Computing and Data Analytics: the Case Study of Electrospindle 4.0

Francesco Leotta[iD], Jerin George Mathew[iD], Massimo Mecella[✉][iD], and Flavia Monti[iD]

Sapienza Università di Roma, Rome, Italy
{leotta,mathew,mecella,monti}@diag.uniroma1.it

**Abstract.** Industry 4.0 represents the last evolution of manufacturing. With respect to Industry 3.0, which introduced the digital interconnection of machinery with monitoring and control systems, the fourth industrial revolution extends this concept to sensors, products and any kind of object or actor (thing) involved in the process. The tremendous amount of data produced is intended to be analyzed by applying methods from artificial intelligence, machine learning and data mining. One of the objective of such an analysis is Zero Defect Manufacturing, i.e., a manufacturing process where data acquired during the entire life cycle of products is used to continuously improve the product design in order to provide customers with unprecedented quality guarantees. In this paper, we discuss the design choices behind a Zero Defect Manufacturing system architecture in the specific use case of spindle manufacturing.

**Keywords:** Zero defect manufacturing · Industry 4.0. · Artificial intelligence · Cloud computing

## 1 Introduction

In recent years, manufacturing processes have undergone several changes to meet the ever increasing demand of customers for highly personalised and high quality products. Actually, conventional production strategies and methodologies, which have been successfully applied in the past, are impractical in the modern industrial setting [1], thus requiring more ones. Recent technological advances, such as Internet-of-Things (IoT), Cyber Physical Systems (CPSs) and Artificial Intelligence (AI), combined with the growing interest in Industry 4.0, fostered the development of a novel paradigm shift in the production process called Zero Defect Manufacturing (ZDM). This strategy aims at reducing the number of defected products to zero by simultaneously considering production planning, quality management, and maintenance management factors in a *first-time-right* fashion [2]. More specifically, this strategy leverages the huge amount of heterogeneous data generated by a company (e.g., shop floor data, product operational

© The Author(s), under exclusive license to Springer Nature Switzerland AG 2022
J. Horkoff et al. (Eds.): CAiSE 2022, LNBIP 451, pp. 119–125, 2022.
https://doi.org/10.1007/978-3-031-07478-3_10

data, supplier data) to build a self-correcting system to predict and detect product defects before they propagate to downstream stages, and to continuously enhance the product design to improve its quality.

The ZDM methodology was initially defined in the early 1960 s s in the US [3] and was further developed in the following years [4]. Recent advances in the manufacturing field, combined with the data-rich environment of modern companies have fostered a renewed interest in ZDM with a vast literature of surveys, frameworks and methodologies to enable and support ZDM strategies. Psarommatis et al. [1] and Powell et al. [2] provide a literature review and investigate recent trends and perspectives in the ZDM field. Wang et al. [5] propose a general framework for ZDM in which data mining techniques play a key role. Angione et al. [6] describe a ZDM reference architecture for multi-stage manufacturing systems (e.g., automotive and semiconductor manufacturing companies) and finally Magnanini et al. [7] present a layered reference architecture to enable ZDM strategies which also relies on data generated from existing management software such as Enterprise Resource Planning (ERP) and Manufacturing Execution System (MES).

In this paper, we present a specific example of ZDM support strategy in the case of a spindle manufacturing company. Spindles are high-precision electromechanical components mounted on top of machine tools and provide rotation to the tool in order to generate working motion. They feature an external or internal electric motor and in the latter case the term *electrospindle* is used to denote such kind of devices. Spindles are manufactured in a variety of configurations and are deployed in several industrial processes, including milling, drilling or grinding for a wide range of materials, including metal, marble and wood. The *Electrospindle 4.0* project aims at applying ZDM principles in the production of spindles. Main goal is to realize new Zero Defect spindles produced by a Zero Defect production process. An innovative family of spindles is equipped with several sensors and computing capabilities; and a new production line is designed to make it more intelligent. Spindles are a representative examples of manufacturing processes of interest in Industry 4.0. Recent research focused on monitoring spindles and their health status to predict and prevent future failures. Relevant works in this field include [8] which propose a cloud-based architecture for predictive maintenance of spindles using Machine Learning (ML) techniques, and [9] which reviews research on intelligent spindles.

The rest of the paper is organised as it follows. Section 2 describes the proposed approach along with the Electrospindle 4.0 case study and finally Sect. 3 draws conclusions and outlines future works.

## 2  Proposed Spindle ZDM Approach

In this section, we describe in more details the proposed approach to support ZDM in the case of spindle manufacturing. A high-level overview of the methodology is shown in Fig. 1. It consists of three main steps, namely *Data collection*, *Data analytics* and *Optimization*, intended to continuously detect and predict failures and incrementally improve the product design and the assembly line. The proposed approach is currently being adopted in the *Electrospindle 4.0* project.

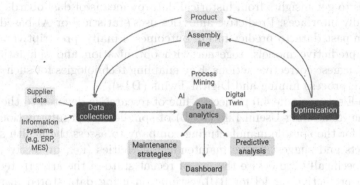

**Fig. 1.** An overview of the proposed approach to support ZDM

## 2.1   Data Collection

In this phase, data generated at different levels of the product lifecycle are collected and sent to a cloud server for subsequent analyses. Four main sources of information can be identified in Fig. 1: *(i)* assembly line data, *(ii)* data generated from the product in the customer environment, *(iii)* data stored in existing management software, such as ERP and MES, and finally *(iv)* data provided by suppliers of raw materials required to build the product. We note that the first two sources of data require the use of highly-digitalized and intelligent products and equipment to sense, collect and send data to a central cloud platform. On the other side, information systems like ERP, MES and Product Lifecycle Management (PLM) provide additional information on the production process and the product design (e.g., production planning and inventory management).

The innovative spindles designed in the *Electrospindle 4.0* project, are capable of automatically collecting several operational parameters coming from the customer environment (e.g., rotation speed, temperature, vibration, power consumption, etc.) and send them to a cloud platform for further processing. Such data will help the spindle manufacturing company to get insights on the product usage patterns from the customer. In addition to that, the production line is composed by new testing machines able to autonomously send the results of performed tests to a central cloud platform to complement data generated from the intelligent spindles and the other data sources mentioned before.

## 2.2   Data Analytics

Data collected from the previous step flows into a data lake provided by a cloud platform for further processing. Data comes from the several sources (as described in Sect. 2.1), however a unique central origin is needed to make analyses. Specifically, three main types of analyses are carried out in this step: *descriptive*, *predictive* and *prescriptive*. Descriptive analytics uses data mining techniques to get insights from historical data by means of dashboards or other user-friendly interfaces. Predictive analytics uses statistical or AI-based models trained on past data to predict future outcomes. Finally, prescriptive analytics leverages predictive models, together with optimization and simulation techniques to suggest corrective actions. Key enabling technologies for such analyses include AI, process mining and Digital Twins (DTs).

In the Electrospindle 4.0 project, a line of research is devoted to the estimation of the Remaining Useful Life (RUL) of spindles. Such information will be beneficial for the spindle manufacturing company to assess the health status of its products and suggest future maintenance activities (i.e., predictive maintenance). Specifically, we devise the use of recent state-of-the-art ML techniques to train a predictive model for RUL estimation using data stored in the data lake and then deploy such a model directly into the spindle (this is a case of edge computing) which in turn will use such reasoning capabilities to generate alerts or warning both to the customers and the spindle manufacturing company. Popular techniques used in the industrial settings for RUL estimation include Auto Encoders (AEs), Deep Belief Networks (DBNs), Convolutional Neural Networks (CNNs) and Recurrent Neural Networks (RNNs) [10–12].

We also devise the use of DTs to create a virtual representation of devices and operations involved in the spindle manufacturing process based on [13], as wells as process mining techniques to model the production line [14] and further improve the automation level of the company. Both of them are crucial in our approach to identify critical issues in the product and the assembly line which may compromise the quality of the spindles manufactured and shipped by the company.

## 2.3   Optimization

Optimization builds on the analyses carried out in the Data analytics phase to support the company in improving both the product design and the assembly line. We note that this requires domain expertise to adequately address design and quality issues which may be highlighted in this step. Indeed, the current step relies on a human-in-the-loop approach to suggest corrective actions.

More specifically, insights from real-time operation data of the product, combined with past failures and faults-related data, should help project managers and designers to identify Critical-To-Quality (CTQ) components of the product and improve their design. Such information should be provided using graphical interfaces, dashboards or any other human-interpretable technique. In addition to this, models and simulations defined in the Data analytics step should also inform company experts about potential bottlenecks, efficiency or quality issues in the assembly line and provide proper steps to address them.

In the Electrospindle 4.0 project, we envision the use of recent machine learning explanation techniques and statistical analyses to extract knowledge from AI models developed in the previous step and find CTQ components of a spindle which mainly affect the RUL of the product. Also, data generated at the shop floor level, combined with DT-based simulations, process discovery and process enhancement techniques, will be used to find bottlenecks and quality related issues in the production process. Finally, we also plan to use Design-for-X [15] based methodologies to build a knowledge base of best practises provided by domain experts as well as general guidelines which will further inform and support designer to improve the manufacturing of spindles.

### 2.4  System Architecture

To support all the required functionalities, a mix of edge, public cloud and private cloud computing [16] has been chosen as system architecture. Machine learning (both training and evaluation) and data mining tasks will be executed using resources from the public cloud (e.g., Azure Machine Learning). Also data from the new family of spindles will be stored in a public cloud. Part of the models will be trained in the public cloud and will be evaluated directly on the spindle using edge computing [17].

A private cloud will be used to store data from information systems of the spindle manufacturing company. These include the ERP, the Customer Relationship Management (CRM) and the MES. A challenge here is the safe and secure interaction between the spindle manufacturing company private cloud and the public cloud solutions that will be used for training purposes. In order to preserve the confidentiality of company's data, data transfer flows must be designed in order to keep the data in the public cloud only at training time.

## 3  Conclusions

In this paper, we outlined an approach to support ZDM strategies based on cloud computing and data analytics. The proposed approach relies on the constant execution of three main steps to incrementally improve the product design and the manufacturing process, which can be summarized as the *collect*, *analyze* and *optimize* loop. We discussed those steps alongside the case study of Electrospindle 4.0, a ZDM initiative involving a spindle manufacturing company together with several industry experts and research institutions. As a future work, we plan to revisit and refine the proposed approach, and to conduct further investigations to evaluate whether the proposed approach can be readily applied to other manufacturing domains which may be significantly different from the spindle manufacturing one.

One of the technical challenge consists in the collection of a dataset big enough to allow for machine (deep) learning training. Unfortunately, the available data could be severely unbalanced. High resolution spindle data will be likely available only in certain phases of the life cycle, namely spindle manufacturing and spindle maintenance, whereas the data coming from the customers

will be at a lower resolution (i.e., one measurement every 10 s), making it difficult to detect short term phenomena. This is due to the necessity of reducing the
data transmitted by customers for their installed spindles. This challenge could
be addressed, in principle, by adding a fog layer to the architecture, but the
consortium (spindle manufacturing company and research institutions) decided
that placing an additional infrastructure at the customer side is not feasible for
security and cost reasons.

**Acknowledgements.** This work has been supported by the Italian MISE project
Electrospindle 4.0 (id: F/160038/01-04/X41).

# References

1. Psarommatis, F., May, G., Dreyfus, P.A., Kiritsis, D.: Zero defect manufacturing:
   state-of-the-art review, shortcomings and future directions in research. Int. J. Prod.
   Res. **58**(1), 1–17 (2020)
2. Powell, D., Magnanini, M.C., Colledani, M., Myklebust, O.: Advancing zero defect
   manufacturing: a state-of-the-art perspective and future research directions. Comput. Ind. **136**, 103596 (2022)
3. Halpin, J.F.: Zero Defects: a New Dimension in Quality Assurance. McGraw-Hill,
   New York (1966)
4. Crosby, P.B., Free, Q.I.: The art of making quality certain. N.Y. New Am. Library
   **17**, 174–83 (1979)
5. Wang, K.S.: Towards zero-defect manufacturing (ZDM)-a data mining approach.
   Adv. Manuf. **1**(1), 62–74 (2013)
6. Angione, G., Cristalli, C., Barbosa, J., Leitão, P.: Integration challenges for the
   deployment of a multi-stage zero-defect manufacturing architecture. In: 2019 IEEE
   17th International Conference on Industrial Informatics (INDIN), vol. 1, pp. 1615–
   1620. IEEE (2019)
7. Magnanini, M.C., Colledani, M., Caputo, D.: Reference architecture for the industrial implementation of zero-defect manufacturing strategies. Procedia CIRP **93**,
   646–651 (2020)
8. Paolanti, M., Romeo, L., Felicetti, A., Mancini, A., Frontoni, E., Loncarski, J.:
   Machine learning approach for predictive maintenance in industry 4.0. In: 2018
   14th IEEE/ASME International Conference on Mechatronic and Embedded Systems and Applications (MESA), pp. 1–6. IEEE (2018)
9. Cao, H., Zhang, X., Chen, X.: The concept and progress of intelligent spindles: a
   review. Int. J. Mach. Tools Manuf. **112**, 21–52 (2017)
10. Wang, Y., Zhao, Y., Addepalli, S.: Remaining useful life prediction using deep
    learning approaches: a review. Procedia Manuf. **49**, 81–88 (2020)
11. Zhai, S., Gehring, B., Reinhart, G.: Enabling predictive maintenance integrated
    production scheduling by operation-specific health prognostics with generative
    deep learning. J. Manuf. Syst. **61**, 830–855 (2021)
12. Zhang, W., Yang, D., Wang, H.: Data-driven methods for predictive maintenance
    of industrial equipment: a survey. IEEE Syst. J. **13**(3), 2213–2227 (2019)
13. Catarci, T., Firmani, D., Leotta, F., Mandreoli, F., Mecella, M., Sapio, F.: A con-
    ceptual architecture and model for smart manufacturing relying on service-based
    digital twins. In: 2019 IEEE International Conference on Web Services (ICWS),
    pp. 229–236. IEEE (2019)

14. Rinderle-Ma, S., Mangler, J.: Process automation and process mining in manufacturing. In: Polyvyanyy, A., Wynn, M.T., Van Looy, A., Reichert, M. (eds.) BPM 2021. LNCS, vol. 12875, pp. 3–14. Springer, Cham (2021). https://doi.org/10.1007/978-3-030-85469-0_1
15. Kuo, T.C., Huang, S.H., Zhang, H.C.: Design for manufacture and design for 'x': concepts, applications, and perspectives. Comput. Ind. Eng. **41**(3), 241–260 (2001)
16. Goyal, S.: Public vs private vs hybrid vs community-cloud computing: a critical review. Int. J. Comput. Netw. Inf. Secur. **6**(3), 20–29 (2014)
17. Chen, J., Ran, X.: Deep learning with edge computing: a review. Proc. IEEE **107**(8), 1655–1674 (2019)

# Digital Twins Approach for Sustainable Industry

Lai Xu[1]([✉]) [iD], Paul de Vrieze[1] [iD], Xin Lu[1] [iD], and Wei Wang[2] [iD]

[1] Department of Computing and Informatics, Bournemouth University, Poole, Bournemouth B12 5BB, UK
{lxu,pdvrieze,xlu}@bournemouth.ac.uk
[2] School of Engineering Science, University of Skövde, 54128 Skövde, Sweden
wei.wang@his.se

**Abstract.** Sustainable industry is a part of The European Green Deal, which aims to achieve the EU's climate and environmental goals based on the circular economy. Digital twins are important technologies for realizing industry 4.0 and related sectors. In this paper, we looked at building the DTs for manufacturing, healthcare and construction industrial sectors in Industry 4.0 architecture to realize a sustainable industry.

**Keywords:** Digital Twins · Sustainable industry · Industry 4.0

## 1 Introduction

Industry 4.0 brings the potential for increased flexibility and efficiency, cost reduction, and increased competitive advantage. Current trends towards Industry 5.0 [1] introduce a complementary view, targeting a sustainable, human-centric, and resilient industry. The notion of Industry 5.0 represents an even more comprehensive strategy on science, technology and innovation aiming for all industries more sustainable while providing effective responses to the economic, technological, and societal rising challenges.

Digital Twins (DTs) describe the effortless integration of data between a physical and virtual object in either direction [2]. Digital Twin is at the forefront of the Industry 4.0/5.0 revolution facilitated through advanced data analytics and the Internet of Things (IoT) connectivity. IoT's data rich environment, coupled with data analytics, provides an essential resource for various problems on the digital-physical interface including but not limited to predictive maintenance and fault detection. In the paper, the initial focus is on manufacturing, healthcare, and construction (addressing e.g., sustainable manufacturing and anomaly detection in patient care) and to look at a potential Industry 4.0 architecture to support sustainable industry through DT technologies.

Manufacturers track, monitor and simulate manufacturing and related processes to save time, reduce costs, become disruption resilient and environmentally friendly [3]. Digital Twins, providing these capabilities, thus have a significant potential for impact within this field [4].

In healthcare and wellbeing (wearable) IoT devices are cheaper and easier to implement than ever before. Based upon this Digital twins of a human, giving real-time analysis of vital signs are now possible. A Digital Twin is used for monitoring and planning treatment and follow up after surgery [5, 6].

J. Horkoff et al. (Eds.): CAiSE 2022, LNBIP 451, pp. 126–134, 2022.
https://doi.org/10.1007/978-3-031-07478-3_11

The construction industry can benefit from Digital Twins by applying them in the development of smart buildings/shopfloors or structures but also as an ongoing real-time prediction and monitoring tool [7, 8]. The use of the Digital Twins and data analytics provides greater quality of Building Information Modelling and predictive maintenance.

A decentralized network comprised of a multitude of ecosystems still yet to be connected and integrated to enable a wide range of applications that contribute to sustainable industry. Building DTs for smart manufacturing, healthcare, and intelligent construction is a necessary step for realizing such sustainable industry. In this paper, we review related DT technologies in manufacturing, healthcare and construction industry in Sect. 2. Section 3 discusses the sustainable industry's objectives and requirements. Section 4 details the architectural solution combining existing implementational architecture. At last, Sect. 5 rounds up the paper with the conclusions.

## 2 Digital Twins in Manufacturing, Healthcare, and Construction Industry

Nowadays, the DT paradigm is becoming more and more permeating in many research domains such as manufacturing, healthcare and construction industry. Since DT concept was proposed, manufacturing has stood out as one of the most promising application fields, attracting substantial attention from both academia and industry. Although there is no unified definition of DT yet, it is well-accept that a DT has to be made by three components: physical entity, virtual entity and their connections [9, 10]. As counterpart of a physical entity, a virtual entity could receive real-time running data of physical entity, analyze it and provide predictive results through simulation that can support decision making. Accordingly, the performance of physical entity could be improved or optimized.

It is clear that bidirectional communication between physical entity and virtual entity is essential to implement a real DT [9]. As a result, Tao et al. proposed that a complete DT should be defined in five dimensions: physical part, virtual part, connection, data, and service [11]. Meanwhile, they listed 9 types of services provided by DT in another work [12]. The researches on DT in manufacturing could be exemplified in different scales, such as equipment [13, 14], workstation [15, 16], production line [17] and production system [18], in terms of these five dimensions as well.

In order to make the CNC machine tool intelligent, Luo et al. [13] applied DT on CNC machine tool to optimize its running mode, reduce its sudden failure probability and improve its stability. Liu et al. [14] investigated the connection modeling and data modeling of CNC machine tool in cyber-physical production system. Two popular information modeling and data exchanging standards for industrial equipment, OPC UA and MTConnect, are successfully applied for digital twins of CNC machine tools. Havard et al. applied DT for the design of human robot collaborative assembly workstation [15].

The ergonomic assessment and safety issue simulation of DT are used to optimize workstation design and regularize the human workers' behavior. Söderberg et al. [16] did an attempt to develop the DT of a sheet metal part assembly line. Their DT can not only use data from individuals to perform real time in-line individual adjustments, but also use data from batches of parts to make adjustment batch wise.

Zhang et al. [17] used DT to optimize the design of hollow glass production line. Benefitting from the powerful simulation of DT, the running information of production line such as the order delivery time, production takt time and production load can be calculated for its iterative optimization.

Fan et al. emphasized the digital twin visualization of flexible manufacturing system [18]. The visualization method of high-value information, for instance, life cycle planning, design, debugging and service stages, was investigated to achieve a lightweight architecture without compromising its functions. As a large amount of work on DT applications in manufacturing exists, the review on the selected literature just provided a systematic view due to space limitation. More details can be found in Ref. [4, 19].

As part of a rise in use of personal health monitoring devices in the form of mobile applications or build-in sensors, which can actively monitor real-time user's vital health parameters, DT technology is being explored to develop fast, accurate and economical solutions to address the massive strain on existing healthcare resources caused by rapid population growth as well as aging populations. Croati et al. present a new healthcare system by integrating DTs with agents and Multi-Agent Systems (MAS) technologies [5]. A preliminary version of a system prototype was developed according to the designed conceptual model and a trauma management process was selected as a case study to evaluate the proposed model. Unfortunately, the paper does not present results that demonstrate the efficiency of the proposed model.

Liu et al. propose a cloud-based healthcare system based on the concept of DT [6]. The patient information, sensed data along with patient symptoms are described by the proposed DT framework to provide real-time monitoring and enabling a personalized healthcare plan with the overall goal of supporting self-management of elderly patients. The results show that a virtual replica of a patient could be an optimal solution for improving healthcare operations.

Rivera et al. present a DT driven model for personalized medical treatments [20], where machine learning and DT serve to track the health status of patients continuously and to allow for virtual evaluation of medical treatments. The definition of internal structures of DT to support precision medicine techniques were elaborated but the system work has not been evaluated in a real case scenario.

Elayan et al. present an intelligent context-aware healthcare system using a proposed (and implemented) DT and IoT framework was proposed to improve healthcare operations [21]. In this framework, a machine learning enabled electrocardiogram (ECG) heart rhythms classifier model was built to diagnose heart disease. The results show that the implemented DT framework with prediction model successfully detects a particular heart condition with quite high accuracy.

Digital twins are broadly applicable, not only in health, but in all kinds of application areas including the construction industry. In the construction industry DT technology has the potential to drive transformation and modernization leading to increased sustainability. Opoku et al. review 22 publications about DT application in the construction industry [7]. The paper provides an overview of the origin, evolution of the concept and industrial applications of DT in the construction industry. It shows that most of the investigated DT applications in the construction industry focused on the design and engineering phase while ignoring the demolition and recovery phases of projects.

Lin and Cheungh propose an advanced monitoring and control system using DT enabled Building Information Modelling (BIM) for underground garage environment management [22]. This paper establishes a real time active model using the combination of BIM and IoTs technologies to provide efficient information during the design of the project. The results show that the designers can make informed decisions by having a complete digital footprint of the project through DT.

Sacks et al. present a data-centric mode of construction management system built on existing concepts of AI and DT [8]. The paper extends the existing understanding of DTs in the construction industry by applying conceptual analysis to derive the four-core information and control concepts to define future development of DT construction systems for the design and construction phases of buildings and infrastructure facilities.

Lu et al. describe a semi-automatic geometric DT system they developed based on images and CAD drawings for facilitating building operation and maintenance management [23]. The paper elaborates on the methodological framework of the proposed semi-automatic geometric DT approach and an office building was employed as a case study to evaluate the proposed system. The results show that DT-assisted operations and maintenance are an effective approach in the operations phase of the building.

## 3 Sustainable Industry

Sustainable industry is a part of The European Green Deal, which aims to achieve the EU's climate and environmental goals based on the circular economy [24, 25]. Sustainability and tackling energy and resource issues (from production to installation, from use and maintenance to disposal or recycling) should be placed at the heart of the combined digital and green transitions early on.

Digital twins are important technologies for realizing industry 4.0 and related sectors. Different DTs can be used for simulating products, materials, and production processes respectively. Another kind of Digital twin is a virtual model of the factory including all elements, i.e., machines, products, and humans, that can be used to simulate the plant operation for improvement or decision making.

Furthermore, the use of industrial data to establish data-based services has potential for further innovation. Digital twins enable sustainable industry where collected industrial data is expected to help improving productivity, flexibility, and resource efficiency through big data for predictive maintenance and fast production system reconfiguration [26].

When a digital twin is used as a virtual model of the factory, it is a model that transvers all parts of the production chain. Such a digital twin can be used to design for disassembly, remanufacturing, and recycling applied in the production life cycle management. In the production life cycle management, lean and green management for resource efficiency can be simulated by using digital twin technologies. A digital twin that connects with a supply chain management, reverse logistics can be designed and evaluated with key performance indicators for the circular economy.

### 3.1    Objectives and Problem Descriptions

In an increasingly digitized world, the physical and digital domains are increasingly intersecting. Digital Twins, originating in NASA, provide a powerful tool that captures this intersection by providing digital representations of physical objects or processes. Not only do Digital Twins provide an interface for the digital world to interact with the physical world, their nature as a digital model of the physical allows for the Digital Twins to be used in ways, for example for simulation, that the physical twin could not.

As the needs of the various cyber physical systems of our modern world are diverse, the form, shape and capabilities of Digital Twins are diverse too, but all are based upon common ingredients: Modeling the physical object to a required fidelity; mediate digital interactions with its physical counterpart; data analytics to maintain consistency with the real-world counterpart; statistics and AI to allow predictions to be made about the future or hidden properties of the physical twin; simulation technology to make predictions on constellations of twinned pairs.

The paper brings together four different types of DTs as well as the even broader application areas. Digital twins, in their nature interdisciplinary, combine various fields of understanding and research. Depending on the purpose of the Digital Twins, different aspects of domain knowledge as well as modeling and simulation approaches is needed.

Some examples of potential technical fields or strategic application domains [22, 27]:

- Digital twins for sustainable manufacturing simulation and real-time interaction with cyber-physical systems
- AI assisted training and assistance systems for optimal factory operation
- Management systems for lifecycle monitoring and operations
- ICT architectures, platforms and standards for industry and logistics 4.0
- High-performance manufacturing systems
- Sustainable, secure and resilient interconnection of all stakeholders and systems
- Cyber-physical production and logistics systems

In short, digital twins can support value creation in different sustainability dimensions. Using digital twins and industrial data generates new business models and new product-services for organizations. Digital twins can be used to improve resource efficiency in a sustainable-oriented decentralized organization through simulation and optimizations. Different digital twins for closed-loop product life cycles and industry symbiosis create value networks. Sustainable production process using digital twins can provide increased sustainability, flexibility, and resiliency. Finally, digital twins could also realize training and competence developments of sustainable industries' needs.

## 4    Architecture

Digital twins are used in the context of a broader industrial ecosystem with supporting IT architecture. Such an architecture is ideally based upon a firm, existing basis, such as provided by FIWARE. FIWARE is an open-source framework for Industry 4.0 as well as a service ecosystem composed of various components, described as Generic

Enablers (GEs) [28]. The GEs can range from different IoT/smart devices, components, and services to big data analysis components for the development of different application solutions. Interoperability and modularity are the key aspects that the FIWARE platform promotes and supports. This offers the industries the ability to easily develop and integrate smart solution for different needs and processes with GE components in a modular manner [28]. In this work, FIWARE is thus adopted for several reasons such as flexibility, interoperability, supporting big data analytics, and by supporting open and industrial standard data model allowing the ease integration of different IoT smart devices, systems.

Based on the objectives identified in Sect. 3.1, digital twins can be implemented for single elements within an organization or multiple digital twins can work together within one organization for optimizing sustainable production processes. Moreover, different digital twins for closed-look product life cycles, and industry symbiosis enable the creation of value networks. Thus, based upon FIWARE, Fig. 1 shows the architecture for DTs for sustainable industries. The proposed architecture can support digital twins within one organization with collected industrial data from different machines, IoTs, etc. as well as support digital twins of crossing different organizations for creating value networks from industry symbiosis.

On the basis of our previous work [29, 30], the architecture is organized in three levels: resource, process and application levels. Sensors, IoTs, items of shopfloor and legacy systems are located at the resource level. Different adapters for sensors, IoTs and machines are collected and managed at the middleware and data modules of the process level. The process level also includes big data analytics and processing engines as well as the FIWARE context broker. The FIWARE context broker provides the communication mechanism with different adapters and the related data sources and storage required for the platform. Our previous work on predictive maintenance provides predictive modules i.e., RUL, predicative maintenance scheduling module, and alert rules module are included at the process level as well. The application level, the predictive maintenance related analysis and monitoring services are supported.

From a common basis and point of synergy, the four different digital twin application areas enhance and bring together our existing expertise [25]. The four digital twins will be developed in the applications level. One manufacturing digital twin will demonstrate improving resource efficiency in a sustainable-oriented decentralized organization. One manufacturing digital twin will extend value networks, i.e., horizontal logistic and production process integration. We explore the visualization and monitoring of manufacturing processes to enhance sustainability and resilience of production and supply chains through digital twin technologies.

One digital twin for lean predictive planning provides shopfloor construction planning capabilities. We explore Building Information Management, an enabler of information delivery and visualization platform that integrates the stakeholders in the supply chain. Given that it has the potential to provide a virtual replica of the physical facility and facilitate vital product information, it naturally serves as a Digital Twin platform, a vital source of information for the proposed project to improve the construction processes from the lean perspective. The digitization of the construction will make the process efficient and effective while retaining the flexibility inherent to this lean approach.

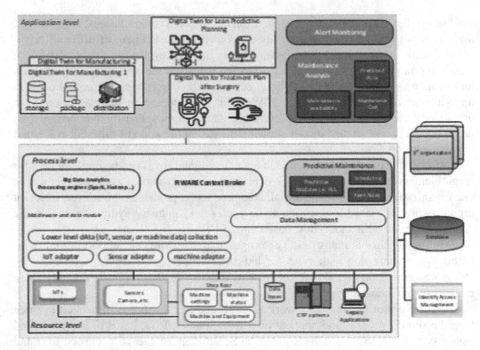

**Fig. 1.** Architecture for supporting sustainable industry

The digital twin for treatment plan enables the improved provision of treatment plans after surgery. We will explore with a biotechnology Ltd. and an obstetrics and gynecology hospital the synergy effect of cutting-edge IT technologies, medical and human factors to create a customized treatment plan to improve patients' quality of life and recovery after surgery (through customized treatment plans and simulation of options). The four mentioned digital twins share some data collection, data management and some data analysis modules in the proposed architecture.

## 5    Conclusion

The digital twin for treatment plan enables the improved provision of treatment plans after surgery. We will explore with a biotechnology Ltd. and an obstetrics and gynecology hospital the synergy effect of cutting-edge IT technologies, medical and human factors to create a customized treatment plan to improve patients' quality of life and recovery after surgery (through customized treatment plans and simulation of options). The four mentioned digital twins share some data collection, data management and some data analysis modules in the proposed architecture.

Based upon cross-disciplines research carried on within the work, the individual DTs cross application domains will be implemented to provide a wide impact through:

- Providing demonstrations for Digital Twin technology for four areas, i.e. building plans, manufacturing, supply chain, and medical treatment.

- Working with real-world cases and individual organizations, sharing the technologies across and developing shared platforms.
- Disseminate to and extend our work with local authorities and businesses.
- Evaluate Digital Twin public health impact in working environments.
- Plans with local hospitals and a public health team providers to develop and evaluate Digital Twins for patient treatments and recovery.

# References

1. EU Homepage. https://ec.europa.eu/info/research-and-innovation/research-area/industrial-research-and-innovation/industry-50_en. Accessed 14 Mar 2022
2. Grieves, M., Vickers, J.: Digital twin: mitigating unpredictable, undesirable emergent behavior in complex systems. In: Kahlen, F.-J., Flumerfelt, S., Alves, A. (eds.) Transdisciplinary perspectives on complex systems, pp. 85–113. Springer, Cham (2017). https://doi.org/10.1007/978-3-319-38756-7_4
3. Fuller, A., Fan, Z., Day, C., Barlow, C.: Digital twin: enabling technologies, challenges and open research. IEEE Access 8, 108952–108971 (2020)
4. He, B., Bai, K.J.: Digital twin-based sustainable intelligent manufacturing: a review. Adv. Manuf. 9(1), 1–21 (2021)
5. Croatti, A., Gabellini, M., Montagna, S., Ricci, A.: On the integration of agents and digital twins in healthcare. J. Med. Syst. 44(9), 1–8 (2020)
6. YingLiu, L.Z., et al.: A novel cloud-based framework for the elderly healthcare services using digital twin. IEEE Access 7(2019), 49088–49101 (2019)
7. Opoku, D.G.J., Perera, S., Osei-Kyei, R., Rashidi, M.: Digital twin application in the construction industry: a literature review. J. Build. Eng. 40, 102726 (2021)
8. Sacks, R., Brilakis, I., Pikas, E., Xie, H.S., Girolami, M.: Construction with digital twin information systems. Data-Centric Engineering, 1 (2020)
9. Cimino, C., Negri, E., Fumagalli, L.: Review of digital twin applications in manufacturing. Comput. Ind. 113, 103130 (2019)
10. Tao, F., Zhang, H., Liu, A., Nee, A.Y.: Digital twin in industry: state-of-the-art. IEEE Trans. Industr. Inf. 15(4), 2405–2415 (2018)
11. Tao, F., Zhang, M., Nee, A.Y.C.: Digital Twin Driven Smart Manufacturing. Academic Press, Cambridge (2019)
12. Tao, F., Cheng, J., Qi, Q., Zhang, M., Zhang, H., Sui, F.: Digital twin-driven product design, manufacturing and service with big data. Int. J. Adv. Manuf. Technol. 94(9–12), 3563–3576 (2017). https://doi.org/10.1007/s00170-017-0233-1
13. Luo, W., Hu, T., Zhang, C., Wei, Y.: Digital twin for CNC machine tool: modeling and using strategy. J. Ambient. Intell. Humaniz. Comput. 10(3), 1129–1140 (2018). https://doi.org/10.1007/s12652-018-0946-5
14. Liu, C., Vengayil, H., Lu, Y., Xu, X.: A cyber-physical machine tools platform using OPC UA and MTConnect. J. Manuf. Syst. 51, 61–74 (2019)
15. Havard, V., Jeanne, B., Lacomblez, M., Baudry, D.: Digital twin and virtual reality: a co-simulation environment for design and assessment of industrial workstations. Prod. Manuf. Res. 7(1), 472–489 (2019)
16. Söderberg, R., Wärmefjord, K., Carlson, J.S., Lindkvist, L.: toward a digital twin for real-time geometry assurance in individualized production. CIRP Ann. 66(1), 137–140 (2017)

17. Zhang, H., Liu, Q., Chen, X., Zhang, D., Leng, J.: A digital twin-based approach for designing and multi-objective optimization of hollow glass production line. IEEE Access **5**, 26901–26911 (2017)
18. Fan, Y., et al.: A digital-twin visualized architecture for flexible manufacturing system. J. Manuf. Syst. **60**, 176–201 (2021)
19. Lu, Y., Liu, C., Kevin, I., Wang, K., Huang, H., Xu, X.: Digital Twin-driven smart manufacturing: connotation, reference model, applications and research issues. Robot. Comput-Integr. Manuf. **61**, 101837 (2020)
20. Rivera, L.F., Jiménez, M., Angara, P., Villegas, N.M., Tamura, G., Müller, H.A.: Towards continuous monitoring in personalized healthcare through digital twins. In: Proceedings of the 29th Annual International Conference on Computer Science and Software Engineering, pp. 329–335 (2019)
21. Elayan, H., Aloqaily, M., Guizani, M.: Digital twin for intelligent context-aware IoT healthcare systems. IEEE Internet Things J. **8**(23), 16749–16757 (2021)
22. Lin, Y.C.P., Cheung, W.F.: Developing WSN/BIM-Based environmental monitoring management system for parking garages in smart cities, J. Manag. Eng. **36**(3), 04020012 (2020)
23. Lu, Q., Chen, L., Li, S., Pitt, M.: Semi-automatic geometric digital twinning for existing buildings based on images and CAD drawings, Autom. ConStruct. **115**, 103183 (2020)
24. Machado, C.G., Winroth, M.P., Ribeiro da Silva, E.H.D.: Sustainable manufacturing in Industry 4.0: an emerging research agenda. Int. J. Prod. Res. **58**(5), 1462–1484 (2020)
25. CSREUROPE. https://www.csreurope.org/our-campaign. Accessed 14 Mar 2022
26. Waibel, M.W., Steenkamp, L.P., Moloko, N., Oosthuizen, G.A.: Investigating the effects of smart production systems on sustainability elements. Procedia Manuf. **8**, 731–737 (2017)
27. Stock, T., Seliger, G.: Opportunities of sustainable manufacturing in industry 4.0. Procedia CIRP **40**, 536–541 (2016)
28. FIWARE: FIWARE Components. https://www.fiware.org/developers/catalogue/. Accessed 14 Mar 2022
29. Sang, G.M., Lai, X., Vrieze, P., Bai, Y.: Towards predictive maintenance for flexible manufacturing using FIWARE. In: Dupuy-Chessa, S., Proper, H.A. (eds.) CAiSE 2020. LNBIP, vol. 382, pp. 17–28. Springer, Cham (2020). https://doi.org/10.1007/978-3-030-49165-9_2
30. Sang, G.M., Xu, L., de Vrieze, P.: A predictive maintenance model for flexible manufacturing in the context of industry 4.0. Frontiers in big Data **4**, 1–23 (2021)

# Author Index

Printed in the United States
by Baker & Taylor Publisher Services